D1580157

NO APPLAUSE IN CHURCH

By the same Author

I Remember Karrigeen

I Remember Maynooth

No Applause in Church

By

NEIL KEVIN

CLONMORE & REYNOLDS LIMITED

DUBLIN

Nihil obstat :   CHRISTOPHORUS RYAN, D.D., Censor deputatus
Imprimatur :   JEREMIAS, Archiepiscopus Cassiliensis
20th August, 1947.

Made and Printed in Eire by
HELY'S LIMITED, DUBLIN
for
CLONMORE & REYNOLDS, LTD.
First Published, October 1947

CONTENTS

"A refinement and correction, such as piety often stands in need of, a help, not so much to religious belief in a world of doubt, as to the maintenance of the religious mood amid the interests of a secular calling."

So wrote Pater, referring to the "Religio Medici". Though it suggests a kind of profundity and grandiloquence such as the reader is not going to encounter in these pages, I have been induced to use Pater's quotation because it happens to suggest what I think is the general drift of my book and saves the reader, and myself, from a longer preface that might not tell any more.

I

No Applause in Church

IN "BARCHESTER TOWERS", when the Rev. Mr. Arabin is about to preach, the novelist holds up the story to reflect upon the whole business of young men preaching to older men. "It often surprises us", Trollope goes on, "that very young men can muster courage to preach for the first time to a strange congregation. Men who are as yet but little more than boys . . . ascend a rostrum high above the heads of the submissive crowd . . . It seems strange to us that they are not stricken dumb by the new and awful solemnity of their position . . ."

Some of us, from time to time, may have found ourselves thinking the same thing. Resting on our own greater maturity we will have considered too much the green years of the preacher and lost sight of the fact that the young man does not have to preach his own ideas but the Gospel. As if anticipating Trollope and ourselves, Paul of Tarsus long ago struck a blow for the young men. "Do not let anyone," he said to Timothy, "think the less of you for your youthfulness."

The majority of the congregation, however, are not likely to be unduly worried by the age of the preacher. If there is going to be comment on the preacher theirs will be of a more obvious, but also more valuable, kind. The strain of it is familiar, running something like this:

We care not whether the preacher ascending the pulpit before us be young or old. We accept the message he has come to deliver. But we are not without some views of our own about how he delivers it. One or two ideas in particular strike us continually about preaching—we, the congregation, who Sunday after Sunday gather ourselves for the sermon, patient, docile (we think), hoping for the best.

This is to be our constructive criticism, not our grievance. When we have said our say we shall remember our place and go on listening with our accustomed docility.

We are, in fact, somewhat proud of our record as the audience. We have been heroic after our fashion. We have always disapproved of our neighbour's yawn and endeavoured to suppress our own, or at least keep it from being too noticeable. We have not slept, when we slept, without making some sort of struggle to keep awake. We derive some consolation from the thought that the association between sermons and sleep has a long history, going back as far as Eutychus, the young man who was "overcome by deep sleep" while Saint Paul was preaching. And because it puts us in such good company we treasure the case of the bishop.

The bishop fell asleep during the sermon at Tenebrae. The sermon ended, and the bishop slept on. Awakened at the conclusion of the service by the ritualistic rapping on the books, he cried out indignantly, "Please, gentlemen, no applause in church."

Preachers, we imagine, are not necessarily as innocent as they sometimes look; and while the head bowed in sleep can look very like the head bowed in acquiescence, we are never sure that we get away with it. But, joking apart, we freely admit that we are not at our best in church. More skill and pains are required to hold our attention to an edifying discourse than to one that has nothing to do with edification. The preacher has every right to assume that we are always on the point of falling asleep. It will be wise for him frequently to assume that we have already fallen asleep.

If this should seem an extreme assumption, it is still preferable to the other assumption that we shall remain awake under any provocation.

We find that earnestness in the preacher is not enough. His very earnestness, if it be not accompanied by other excellences, may only intensify monotony.

Frequently we have been impressed by the determination with which the preacher opened his discourse. We have made a corresponding effort to be worthy of his spirit. We have seen in him the signs that he spent much time since last Sunday preparing this sermon for us. And still the attention has flickered and died in us, and we have come to with a start to find that he has finished.

In so far as there is failure we believe the chief cause of it to be a false style which the preacher uses. His mode of expression is not sufficiently his own. He has a great chance of holding us if he speaks plain, if he speaks out of himself. This he does not do. He takes on a style. He slips away from us. Words come between him and us. A medium is interposed. He recedes from us. From the effects of his gestures and his very excitement we are removed. Each time he calls us 'Dear Brethren' he gets farther away from us. We lose interest not because he is speaking of things that do not interest us, but because he is speaking in a language we do not use.

Even before the microphone appeared in the church the Age of Oratory had passed. At the beginning of this century it needed no very quick perception to see that grandiloquence was going out of favour and a plainer style was coming in. That the change from ornate to plain was a bad thing many will say, pointing to the change as an index of a general decline in our civilization. Which style is the best style according to the ageless standard is a question of much interest. But for the preacher with his message to deliver it is not so important a question as: Which style will the people listen to? So many cling still to the old style and speak as if the thing for the preacher of to-day was to model himself on Burke and Pitt.

Outside the church we have grown intolerant of Oratory. Occasionally we come upon a shred of that former glory surviving in the speech of an antique chairman, whose failure to talk the contemporary idiom we forgive him—and this even with some reluctance—because of his advanced age. Inside the church, of course, the story is different. There our influence, as the audience, has not been brought to bear. And, because we have so consistently refrained from anything approaching a manifestation of impatience, the dead language still passes there for the living.

We in the pew believe we see the preacher's peculiar difficulty in this matter. A traditionalist by his calling he will not be the first to acknowledge the decay of the old glory. His sermon books are written by the great men of the past. He can do no better, he thinks, than take a deep breath and periodize as they did.

Our long experience of this oratorical style, which, as we say, we now encounter principally in the church, has made us rather sharp in detecting its weaknesses. Our main objection to it is that inferior forms of it are too easily acquired. That preachers may see the weakness of this style the more clearly we ask them to observe it in that sphere in which, next to that of the church, it most flourishes—the sphere of politics. They will find something illustrative in the parliamentary candidate who has a very great distaste for public speaking and is forced to the platform by the necessity of an election. In this man's extreme need he clutches at the oratorical style. He does so because only by the adopting of it can he appear to be saying something when in reality he is saying nothing.

Those with a flair for writing letters of an unnecessary character to the provincial papers turn as one man to this ornate, flamboyant style.

These two are undoubtedly the lowest forms of rhetorical life. But we think it right to remind our preachers that every sort of failure at the rhetorical style sounds too much like these. Our ears are grown suspicious of the polysyllable and the raised voice. For better or for worse we associate sincerity with the plain style and with it alone. Preachers may sigh at this but they have no option. They may not be conscious to themselves of attempting any style—and certainly not, they would protest, the ornate style—but we who have such an unique opportunity of knowing must report that they include freely enough in their sermons a selection of those same devices that have come down from the 'palmy days' of oratory.

Before the preacher begins his sermon, he will tell us in plain and precise words that the October collection will be made on next Sunday, or that there will be Confirmation in the parish on the third Sunday of May. There is perfect contact between his mind and ours. Then he begins to preach. He makes a change of key. He says: "I would ask you, dearly beloved brethren, to meditate . .". Automatically we rearrange ourselves in our seats, seeking more comfort, and take a chance with distraction or sleep.

II

The Unattractiveness of Spiritual Books

WHILE SLEEPING OVER THE SERMON is the subject of many a staid old joke, sleeping over the pious book has gone with comparatively little publicity. This is probably because it is done mostly in private. But many an honest—and holy—man has admitted that it is his practice always to keep a pious book by his bedside to make him sleep. Fully allowing for the weakness of the reader's flesh in these instances, one is still tempted to compute the author's contribution to the state of sleep. Temerariously, I have gone a stage further and undertaken, as follows, to show how the readers of spiritual books might (in their worst moments, perhaps) write to the authors of them:

Firstly, in fairness to everyone, let us say to what extent we are readers of spiritual books and thus show on what we base the comments which follow. We can speak only with the authority of one a little better versed than the average reader. We are not students or assessors of this literature, but we are aware of its general style. We have a 'gentleman's knowledge' of it. If our knowledge is not comprehensive, we still think our familiarity with it sufficient to speak in general terms of it as a class of writing.

Our first impression is that authors of spiritual books have not at any time suffered enough correction. The notion seems to have prevailed that because these books treat of things holy that they themselves are thereby to be treated as things sacred and not to be subjected to any adverse criticism. As if the religious sign or emblem which the book wears on its outside were a protective charm, the reviewer holds his hand, and the bad workmanship of the author is let pass out of deference to the theme he has chosen. There is no mill through which spiritual writing must pass equivalent to that through which secular writing must make its way. The result is a low standard of work. That study of technique with a view to getting the highest degree of effectiveness—a study which is so noticeable amongst contending novelists, for instance—shows not at all amongst spiritual writers. The theme must make up for everything—which is not fair to the theme.

Redundancy dulls the whole field of this literature. An author will repeat himself manifestly from book to book, and repeat himself within the same book. It is difficult not to have the impression that we are for ever reading the same book under an array of different titles. Nor can we help contrasting the authors of spiritual classics of times past, who were able to say all they had to say about the spiritual life in one or two books, with the spiritual writers of these times who require so many books to complete our edification.

Good intentions are not, of course, questioned, but good intentions are not enough. Reviewers of spiritual books could help us greatly by saying so. Their reticence is bad for religion. How entirely unaccustomed we are to finding a reviewer saying that the Rev. John Brown's book on the Sacraments suffers from an extraordinarily clumsy arrangement of its parts and is rendered almost unreadable by a tortuous style. Or how surprised we should be if a reviewer were to take the normal liberty of a reviewer of secular books and convey to us politely, but unmistakably, that Sister Mary Pius's book on the Seven Gifts of the Holy Ghost was unbelievably bad. Such discouragements are necessary for the general good: we all know what terrible books the Rev.

John Brown and Sister Mary Pius will write if they are not discouraged.

Not unnaturally, spiritual writers address most of their books to those in some special way dedicated to a religious life. Perhaps, it would be better if they divided their energies more evenly between ourselves, the plain men, and that other more select and limited audience. This however is not a point for us to press. But we would ask them, when they write for us, to keep in mind our real state and our real needs, and to disengage their attention more than they do from those who live the cloistered life.

Here is a small point, seemingly, but one of unsuspected importance. Could not the spiritual writer, when he writes a book for us, arrange with the publisher to present it with the appearance of an ordinary book, and not give it the stamp of a book that should be read only in a church or by a person wearing some kind of religious habit? Why not give us the thing less obviously labelled? Why not let the appearance of his book suggest that it is as normal a thing (at least) to write about spiritual as about secular affairs. Many amongst us are chilled, or even oppressed, by the very outside of spiritual books. We feel that this need not be so. Actually the spiritual writer is writing about something of concern and of interest for every Christian, something that was the burden of the plain man's conversation in an older world. The extent to which it is ever to be so again depends quite a bit on him and his book.

We must report that most of the spiritual literature which is aimed at us directly or indirectly does not commend itself to us. It is not to our taste. To us it does not seem normal enough or realistic enough. It is over-concerned with the mystical aspect of religion. The books are all for *students* of the spiritual life; they are abstract and theoretic. The writers of them who are not professional theologians leave on us the impression that they would like to be considered very respectable amateurs.

We do not deny that we are a difficult public for the spiritual writer, we men who are religious only in a plain way, who are making our way to the next world without having turned our back on this one. We are aware of a sort of inborn reluctance in us towards cultivation of a higher spiritual way—we know that reluctance comes from our childish misconception that sanctity is a weakener of our native hardiness, which we over-prize. We know of our tendency to over-use the word 'piosity', and to give the name 'sanctimoniousness' to that which is really sanctity. These things we know and allow for; and yet we urge against the general body of spiritual writers that they leave about their books a discouraging air of unreality, due to the fact that they have, or endeavour to have, or inadvertently give the impression of having, such an exclusive interest in the next world that they lose sight of the actualities of this one.

You are, O Spiritual Writers—if we may take the liberty of addressing you—like all authors, hidden from us behind your books. You are more hidden, even. We are prepared for this; your subject prepares us for it. But in so far as you do show yourselves—we speak in general terms—we feel bound to tell you that we do not find you particularly interesting. Your detachment we are prepared for, but we are not prepared for what we can only call your lack of humanity, your lack of relish for humanity. We cannot help feeling that we would not like to spend too much time with you.

The atmosphere of your books we find too rarified, your spirituality is too refined. You speak of things like 'getting rid of Self' with a casualness which amazes us. For you it is a mere preliminary, and as likely as not, you will base your treatise on the assumption that this is accomplished with finality. St. Paul by the way, did not go so lightly over this problem of the two laws. It takes much from your effectiveness that you are not as conscious of the actualities of this life as you ought to be. You are too removed. You are too apt to write as if you were addressing the disembodied soul. You are too apt for speculation. You may quote the wise saying that it is better to feel compunction than know its definition. But in the very next paragraph you are likely to involve us in a discussion as to whether prayer is an act of the intellect or the will. The great Teresa writing on prayer is easier going for us because her sense of proportion is better. Like the writer of the *Imitation* (another consolation for plain men) she keeps the 'science' of the spiritual life in its place.

We are, we repeat, a difficult public for the spiritual writer. Still we feel he should be able to do much better for us than he does. To succeed he will have to stand closer to us than he does. We, with our one foot so firmly on the ground, have our own sort of 'spiritual life,' though it does not seem to merit such a description at all. We know that it is not merely when we are attending the annual retreat that we must have in mind that the point and purpose of this life is to serve God. The logical result of this line of reflection would be an embracing of the religious life. We see that, too. But logic does not do that to everyone, and such 'conversion' is not, in the way of things, necessary for salvation.

See us for what we are, is our first advice to you who write for our edification. We are the great majority. To be effective in your general aim you must somehow reach us; otherwise you will just go on, as you are, writing for one another, writing within a small ring, making a corner in the counsels of perfection. Remember that a great saint, when asked what he would do if it were announced to him during a game of chess that he was about to die, replied that he would finish the game of chess. You have quoted this with approval, but you give every sign that you yourselves would not wait to finish the game.

Think of us as resembling the saint at least in this that we would wait to finish the game. We are a varied mass hopefully moving on to Heaven, but at a pace that you will think slow or even sluggish. Have patience with us if we are not as gifted or as illuminated as you who are wholly dedicated. We read the signs and hear the admonitions according to our state. Christ's frequent admonitions to us to be always ready is taken by us, as we go on living our multifarious lives, to mean a normal state of readiness, not one to be arrived at by occasional impetuosities or grand-scale heroics, not by beating the breast hard enough on one day to do for a week.

We do not believe this way of ours is in conflict with the spiritual principle that one must be always advancing or one is falling back. The thought that the purpose of our lives is to serve God does not turn us back from the football match or the cinema any more than it turns us back from the mission. The chances of finding anything at the football match to remind us of our last end are admittedly not high. But there we are, and to write a good spiritual book for us, you must keep in mind how much the football match means to us.

Our desire, here and now, is to convey to you some idea of the quality or temper of our spirituality. Our 'attitude' towards our last end we have mentioned because it must be the shortest and simplest key to us. Preparedness for the next life we take to be a normal state, a human rather than superhuman bearing of ourselves. We are sure we seem more thoughtless than we are, and that we appear to take shelter in the crowd from our sense of responsibility more than actually we do. As we see it, the journey towards eternity is like setting out on a train journey, along with many like us, meaning to get to a certain place and not to any other place. At every moment of our journey we have not present to our minds our destination. But our destination is all the time our over-riding interest, a fact so clearly revealed by the first faint hint or far-off suggestion that the train is travelling in the wrong direction.

In all this you may think that we have made rather a fuss about ourselves. Our reason for doing so is that we have for some years suffered an accumulation of feeling on this matter. Without going into statistics, we have formed an idea that this present century has seen an increased industry in the writing of spiritual books, but has shown no increased effectiveness on the part of authors to write the books we want. The first cause of ineffectiveness is, as we have said, a wrong outlook of the writers, a wrong view of us. The other cause is to be found, we are convinced, in inferior workmanship.

III

The 'Clerical Style'

A REVIEWER OF A RECENT biography of a churchman, written by a cleric, included amongst his praises of it that it was not written in the 'clerical style.' The publishers quoted the reviewer's remark in their advertisements. It is, obviously, the sort of assurance that commends a book on a religious theme to a wider public.

'Clerical style' may be a somewhat vague phrase, but none of us are so innocent as not to have a general idea of the meaning of it. One thing is certain, the clerical style is a dull style. We may go farther and say it is a forbidding style. We associate with it an unrelieved rigidity, an embalmed stateliness, an ecclesiastical odour. The ordinary man, the average reader—the plain people—feel that nothing written in it could possibly be written for them, and they are somewhat depressed to think that there are any people who can find it agreeable.

From the lives of the saints, which we know could interest us enormously, we are kept away by the 'clerical style.' The subject is one so often capable of being treated with fine liveliness, the book is so often dull and insipid. The link by which we are capable of being made one with the saint—our common nature—is in the book quite ignored. We get philosophy, but not psychology. The saint is a dead man right from the beginning. The author may think he is writing the saint's *Life*, but he is in reality only using him as an illustration of his own views about the 'religious life.' The publisher of the book, or some mechanical reviewer of it, may assert—with a view to exciting us into buying it—that it is as thrilling as any novel. But we who fall asleep over it know better.

Once in a while someone writes a spiritual book as if he were not writing a spiritual book and the sales rival the popular novel. This does not happen nearly often enough. The mass of readers who are out of sympathy with, or even repelled by, the usual style of the spiritual book, and who are not moved to overcome their repugnance from considerations arising out of a higher vocation, must make their way to Heaven on novels alone.

The prevailing style in religious books—the clerical style —is archaic. The writers of it are centuries behind their readers. Novelists of to-day do not do anything so absurd as to try to have a style by imitating what would have been considered 'the graces of composition' in the early seventeenth century. Spiritual writers do. St. Francis of Sales wrote *The Devout Life* in a style that was in vogue in his day. That style is not now a favoured style; it is considered too precious. It is the sort of writing that was given the labels 'euphuistic' and 'metaphysical' in England. That quaint and over-precious style is as definitely out of favour in the twentieth century as it has been at any time since its wane.

Quite naturally, no doubt, Saint Francis wrote: "If charity be the milk, devotion is the cream, if charity be a plant, devotion is its flowers, if charity be a rich balm, devotion is its odour; yea, the odour of sweetness, which comforts men and rejoices angels." But such a manner of expression the spiritual writer of to-day cannot claim to use *naturally*. In him it is an affectation, and he uses it at his peril.

The elaborate simile was considered good in the seventeenth century before prose was sufficiently disengaged from the way of poetry. Saint Francis was holding his own with those considered effective writers when he wrote: "As the queen bee never goes into the fields without being surrounded by all her subjects, so charity, the queen of the virtues, never enters the heart without bringing all the other virtues in her train, exercising and disciplining them, as a captain does his soldiers." Very little reflection shows that when people of these times want to make the point here made about charity, this is certainly not the way they are accustomed to make it.

A generation that cooks with gas and goes to the pictures twice a week is out of touch with the habits of the bee. Our generation has brought its own language upon it; whether it be poorer or richer than that of times past, it is certainly not the language we find in very many present-day spiritual writers. The reader does not go far amongst the latter before he is aware of a diction that would have served all the purposes of the most eccentric of the English Metaphysical poets. The vocabulary of the Metaphysicals is here complete. Havens and ransoms, diseases and remedies, balms and odours, spices and turtles—they flourish in the spiritual book when they flourish nowhere else.

Little value is set upon plain speaking. Everything must be translated into grandiloquence. Out of this conception of how to treat a sublime subject spring such expressions as: "From the pharmacy of his unfathomed wisdom he drew the remedy." The equivalent, in writing, to so much of our church statuary is attained. From constant straining after grandiloquence the bad style becomes stereotyped. Its unreality pervades the simplest and most casual context. It is not thought impressive enough to say that a man is too fond of something: it must be stated that he 'nurtures an inordinate affection for it.'

Special protest must be made against the spiritual writer's way of mixing the materials of prose and poetry, against his failure to see that the standard of excellence in the one will not do for the other. Instead of quoting from the poetic books of the Old Testament, when it is fitting to do so, he will scatter the richness of their diction inconsiderately over his pages. Words with power in them to send the mind back through thousands of years of history will be found miserably attended, upon the page, homesick and forlorn like the Israelites in their wanderings. Or so they will seem to the eye that sympathetically delays over them. Modern man, suspicious of poetry and reared upon the newspaper, whose only theory of language is to call a spade a spade—this modern man, when he is aware that it is the business of his soul to seek God will be slow to see the force of, and will only be made uncomfortable by, the writer insisting on calling him a hart.

Modern man has not the same stomach for simile and allegory that his ancestors had. Present day capacity for figurative language is less than in most former ages. This they cannot afford to overlook who write for us, whether they write of religious or secular matters.

For instance, a certain 'tact' in the writer is necessary if such an expression as 'Spouse of Christ' is to be used successfully. There must be more discrimination than to use it as a rough-and-ready, fifty-fifty equivalent of the word, Church. Some degree of poetry must have been achieved in a context before its use is justified. In an everyday, purely matter-of-fact prose context it will sound unreal, because in everyday language the word *spouse* is not used. It is easy to test this by trying to imagine a man saying seriously, "My spouse has a bad cold" or "My spouse has a handicap of fifteen." In so far as the word has any vitality in everyday language, it is for the humour that arises from its being an archaic word, or reserved for poetry. No more than any

other user of the language, the spiritual writer cannot afford
to overlook facts like this.

A further deadening quality of the spiritual writer's style
is a straining after the infinite in expression. Ever and always he is marching up troops of limping superlatives. They
fail him, for they must; and he covers his retreat with the
word which includes defeat, the word *ineffable*. Hardly any
word has been called on so much as *ineffable*, the Latin form
preferred to its English equivalents. Sometimes the spiritual
writer makes the irreparable mistake of beginning with *ineffable;* for, despite the plain meaning of the word, he does
not leave it at that, but goes on tediously lining up phrase
with phrase as if he imagines that by repeating himself often
enough he will make plain a wonder or get at the heart of
a mystery.

It is inadequate consolation for us to know that he means
well. He will only do harm until he learns that there is more
reverence and impressiveness in reticence. And how thoroughly dull this superlative style is. Instead of strength there
is feebleness, sound instead of meaning, no vitality in the
composition but death from too much fat about the heart.
We are not aware of the writer *saying* anything to us. There
is no progress in his thought. A dreamlike procession of old
familiar shapes and sounds of words goes on around us and
we know that it can go on for ever. The 'limitless sea of unspeakable torture and extremest agony' is followed in good
time by the spectacle of those failing to 'plumb the depths
of the ocean of divine benignity.' The thing is endless.

In this bad style the adjective is never withheld. The
nouns are oppressed until all the life is gone out of them.
Were we to count up the superfluous adjectives we should
have isolated one of the chief causes of the general distaste
of this class of writing. What a relief it is to turn from the

adjectival style of the dull spiritual book to the language of the Gospels and the Acts where everything is transparent, where the mind is honestly engaged by things and not by words, and noun after noun meets the eye standing impressive, alone.

IV

On putting the Second Commandment First

PARTIAL KNOWLEDGE AND ADHERENCE to the gospel of Christianity produces strange anomalies in religious practice. A common anomaly is the free-lance follower of Christ who has made a selection from the Gospel of those parts which have most appeal for him, the parts in which the ideas of Christ happened to fit in with his own. His underlying conviction is that he has the right to figure things out his own way.

He may be a very good man. His observation may have led him to conclude that his own charity is greater than that of some of the men who have written books to prove him wrong. And in this he may well be right. His conscientiousness within the field of his conviction is admirable. His sincerity too is admirable—though perhaps we would have to say that his own awareness of it is too keen, and prevents the luminosity of real humility.

The free-lance does not want to hear one word more about doctrine. He figures he is alright. He means to go through life with his mind shut—though he does not think of it in this way—and supported by a feeling of satisfaction with his own goodness, which, again, he does not think of as such. It is possible that it is his high-grade sincerity that is most misleading him. For wonderful though this quality be, it is not enough. A man may support half a gospel with a fierceness of spirit that the holder of all of it cannot match. And if he does, he will certainly draw the wrong conclusions.

Christ is this man's hero rather than his God, a Christ according to a particular formula, a Christ of his own creation. The free-lance has a quick eye for injustice. It is certain that in his own sphere he does more than most to prevent it. He is full of honest indignation as he points to enormities in the dealings of those professedly Christian. I meet him here or there, after a game of golf, or in a railway carriage. By some accident or chance the conversation arrives at such considerations. We both warm to the theme. He gets much warmer than I do. I give him his head. I am impressed by the intensity of his conviction concerning those parts of the gospel that are the whole of his. I cannot refrain from comparing him with more orthodox Christians and giving him the benefit of the comparison.

But for all his earnestness and sincerity I begin to grow more and more dissatisfied with his half gospel. The peculiar intensity with which he preaches it makes only more apparent the fact that it is the half and not the whole. Still more he warms to his theme. It is no longer a discussion. This free-lance is a preacher, a reformer. He makes admission that there are, no doubt, better churchgoers than he. But I faintly suspect that he has decided he is none the worse for that.

Friendly, and anxious to save me embarrassment, he defers to my clerical office and makes some apology for preaching to me. His delicate way of glancing at organized religion (though he uses no specific term) amounts to the flattering implication that if all clergymen (he has no concern to differentiate the churches) were like myself, religion (his religion) would prosper despite the mistake (I feel he would use a stronger word) of having 'organized' religion. The compliment makes me uneasy, I may say; because in addition to having it at the expense of my clerical brethren, it is clear from other things he has said that I can hardly qualify for it and retain my banking account.

The free-lance's approach is the temperamental approach to religion. As much of Christianity as will go with a particular outlook or make-up is not only accepted but is given off to others, on little provocation, with eyes dimmed by emotion.

Further, this way is very much conditioned by the 'trend of the times.' For a long time now the free-lance Christian has been concentrating on the second commandment, the love of one's neighbour. The growth of the democratic way in society, the insistence of the propertyless worker on a more equitable sharing of wealth have made the second commandment seem above all things a 'good thing' to the free-lance. More and more, virtue is being made out of necessity. Compassion for the poor has become so considerable in the minds of many, whose social equivalents in the former ages of the world were so unaffected by it, that it is the whole of Christianity for them. That ever-increasing sums of public monies are devoted to relief schemes for the needy and afflicted has put the tax-payer in the way of being able to see himself as the Good Samaritan.

The total abolition of poverty is viewed as life eternal. Whoever thinks it is not is considered (by the free-lance) to have preserved in himself only the worst elements of religion. The first commandment, the love of God, and the worship and manifold service of God which follow from it, are lost sight of in the whole-time concern with the second commandment. This sentimentalism, conceived as the whole of Christianity, thinks it monstrous to build a church while there is a beggar at the gates. The churches—but usually only the churches—are to be sold and the money given to the poor. The time spent in prayer is vain while there is social work to do. The elaborate ritual, the vestments of cloth-of-gold, the temple of adoring stone are waste—and hence worse. God is censured for putting the second commandment second. Once again there is a proposal to sell the pound of right spikenard.

Humanitarianism has its obviously attractive side. It is a dictate of the Christian conscience. The free-lance, however, is disappointed with us because we do not make more of it. For him it is everything. I have the greatest trouble when he has unburdened himself to me in suggesting to him, without needless hurt, that the very thing he preaches may even be a heresy against Christianity. Even while he is flushed with fine and honest feeling about Christian charity and the neglect of brotherly love I must keep my head (which in the heightened atmosphere of love and generosity, which he has created, seems an almost inhuman thing to do) and insinuate that the serving of our fellow man is not the only way of serving God.

Minds noble in their way, noble in so far as the unenlightened mind can be noble, have swept along to this assumption that the second commandment is the whole of Christianity. The unprincipled demagogue who does not scruple to take advantage of his audience by what looks like a display of high motives, and all those zealots preaching social reconstruction at the street corner will include the fallacy in their eloquence. The bitter and unscrupulous ones lean upon it, pointing scornfully to priest and church as if these were the cause of the beggar's distress and their removal the first step in social reform.

One and all of these, in so far as they are honest, are eaten up with the half-gospel of the free-lance. To-day it is preached by the man praising Communism, yesterday it was preached by Ruskin. Ruskin directed his scorn at "the dramatic Christianity of the organ and the aisle." He was not content to say "Look after Lazarus at the door-step"; but must add "get rid of the smoke and the organ pipes, leave the Gothic windows and the painted glass to the pro-perty-man."

Meantime Ruskin and all those Christians of the second commandment neglect Christ's view. When the Founder of Christianity spoke the text of humanitarianism—the parable of the Good Samaritan—He did not omit a reference to the priest neglecting the law of charity, but the reference was made without supplying a text for anti-clerics. It was not Christ who said it was a pity to waste the precious ointment and that it ought to be sold and the money given to the poor. Christ did not preach against the 'organ and the aisle.' Instead, He reverenced the costly temple of Jerusalem as the worshipful offering of His race. He did not say that relief-schemes for the poor should have place before it. He watched the widow contribute her mite in the temple. He noted her great poverty. Still He approved of the offering. This is the point that the Christians of the second commandment keep missing.

V

On being a Sport

THE VERY HIGHEST IMPORTANCE is attached to being a 'sport.' The meaning of the word is not well restricted. It may mean anything from not being a killjoy to the undertaking of the daftest escapades for no better reason than that someone has been found daft enough to propose them. In so far as it is based on such admirable dispositions as unselfishness and good-will the general policy of 'being a sport' is entirely irreproachable.

The thoughtless (so far outnumbering, as they do, the thoughtful) have, however, over-strained the virtue. They have turned it into a sort of hoodoo. They have not stopped until they have brought it about that perfectly normal people engage in what they know to be the most absurd and unwelcome undertakings out of a primitive sort of fear that if they do not so engage they will be visited by some irreparable disfigurement (socially). Tests well outside the range of what is reasonable are for ever being applied to see if one is a sport. The thoughtful weaken before the numerical superiority of the thoughtless and try as hard as they can to make the necessary fools of themselves.

Due to this over-emphasis, the degree of dissipation found in many a scene can be taken as being much higher than those dissipating wish it to be. A 'good time' will be found full of inconveniences and discomforts. To prove this one does not have to refer to a lunatic situation in which some young man, who is having the clothes torn off his back or water poured down inside his shirt, will still grin with un-failing sportsmanship. Much more usual situations will prove it. Many, for instance, who can be found engaged in what is intended to be revelry of one kind or another in the small hours of the morning would much prefer to be in their beds, and they would certainly have gone there hours before if it had not been for their fear of not being thought sports. And ungifted people have the additional fear that, if they lose the reputation of being sports, they will not have much left to recommend them to society. These last can clearly be a very great menace, because, having no accomplishment to ad-vance them in the esteem of their fellows save only the fact that they are sports, they are much inclined to keep up the demonstration. Thus it happens that the lead is often coming from the quarter least fitted to give it.

A few who are singular in that they derive untold satis-faction from not going to bed will cause a whole party of quite normal people to give the illusion that they see point in staying up, when they do not, or even to give the illusion that they are enjoying themselves. The extreme case is that in which no one at all wants to stay up but actually every-body does—and this because a few, who are no such thing, are presumed to be sports of the uncompromising sort by the rest who are, themselves, only pretending to be sports.

The standard set by the few stands there unwelcome to the many. Drinking for instance has its own agreeable standards arising out of the common laws of hospitality and goodfellowship, but the business of being a sport eventually adds a mad ruling of its own. In the face of it a man may have to renounce the conviviality altogether; or give a display of strength of character which, at best, will get only a mixed re-ception; or explain that the physiological fact is that he has a stomach much inferior to the rest of the company. It is even doubtful if it will be allowed to him to be a sport and have an inferior stomach at the same time.

In their bodily recreations men have no hope of escape at all from the hoodoo. Here they are not allowed to grow beyond their schooldays. The old cry 'Be a sport' can make their relaxations miserable to the end of their days. Honouring the code, they rise again and again to the game like beaten boxers. A strange fantastic value is placed on being game to do the thing again and again—and after that just once more, endlessly. A refusal to stop, especially when the reasonableness of stopping becomes more and more manifest, is the required disposition. An awful significance is given to mere endurance.

'Sports' who have played enough, and are well aware of it, will propose that some more be played, and are acceded to by men who would prefer to lie down where they stand (and are truly not fit for much else) because of the old fear. Here the extreme is reached when each believes the other to be bluffing but believes also that the other will find the strain harder than he.

Where this anxiety to be a sport and the thing called 'human respect' (mere) become one it is not easy to say. When the 'sport' mentality is taken outside the domain of purely indifferent acts the bad result may very well be more than inconvenience. In the realm of the spirit one may come to grief from the folly of applying there the 'sport' notion.

As if with a wish to be considered more sporting than the rest, some adopt the style of being less concerned and more reckless about adjusting this life to the next. They aim at a greater spaciousness in action. The reckless way has some virtue in it, to their thinking, just because it is the reckless way. Much, they seem to imagine, will be forgiven to them because they are 'sports.' They are of the impression that a spirit of insubordination becomes them better than it becomes the general run of men. It is their way to scorn calculation and to turn their back flatly on to-morrow. And this is only routine with them. Why not go the whole hog and have the thrill of being fellows who are taking a chance with the next life? To convince others that they are actually being sports of this stature they will naturally have to give some clear indications of it. And so the 'sport' gets out of his depth.

It is not that the sport grows antagonistic to religion, or grows so liberal in his views that the notion of institutional religion makes him irritable. Nothing makes him irritable. In fact, part of his spacious way as a sport is due to his not having any views. It is because he does not use his head much that he has the excessive and unintelligent interest in being a sport that he has. He is not the type who puts on a great air and says how much sermons get him down. He is not the type of the local intellectual who, because he is able to take the measure of the local curate, begins to bear himself as if he had taken the measure of God too. The sport is none of these. He is neither superior nor antagonistic. But he does like, on Saturday night, to make it quite clear in the bar that he will be ready at any hour on Sunday morning for anything. He gets a thrill out of shrugging his shoulders in a certain way to indicate that he is not fussy about the church stuff.

VI

On being a Creature

THE OBVIOUS IMPLICATION of creaturehood is that we *belong*, that we are under obligation, that we owe service. Our logic tends to be bad here. We have a deep understanding of service when it is owed to us, but it is not so when we owe. Men hardly ever look so righteous as when they are claiming the service they have paid for, the service owed to them. They are then a particularly interesting study. They do, really, at such a time seem concerned with the preservation of right order in the universe, they transcend the particular, their concern is ontological. Apart from getting that which is their due, they talk about the 'principle of the thing' more than they do in any other circumstances.

An excessive regard for the right to service which has been paid for is one of the peculiar notes of modern living. Further, modern men pride themselves on having a high rate of insistence. Due, possibly, to too much indiscriminate talking about Psychology, not to be insistent is rated a sign of weakness of character. Those who are not able to make an adequate scene when the whole pound of flesh is not rendered accept themselves for men who suffer from an inferiority complex, and turn for consolation to advertised courses in character-building.

The demand on all sides is, "Service", the service owed, the service paid for. A man will demand it even when he no longer wants it; he will have it because it is due. The rich man pays his pound in the luxury hotel and questions the speed of the bell-hops. The poor man pays his shilling in the theatre, and the management must safeguard itself against him by a note in the programme. Everyman says 'Pay what thou owest,' and throttling is common. Throttling is called being businesslike.

A highly developed sense of rights does not, however, mean an equal sense of obligation, which is why signing on the line has the place it has in human affairs.

The moral is a mile wide. Obligation is fair play but it cuts both ways. Christ used the logic of it when speaking to his disciples. He asked them to consider a plain case. A man does not thank his servant, does he, when the servant has done his day's work in the field? "I think not," said Christ, replying to his own question and using the figure of the understatement. The man rather says to the servant, "Prepare my supper now." Which is the accepted state of things between them, the bond. The bond does not include a vote of thanks. And as the servant to his employer, so is man to his Maker. All his service is owed. It follows from his very status as a creature.

In general, the more complicated the machinery of life becomes the more men are liable to lose sight of their creaturehood. Primitive man stooping at the door of his cave had a better chance of remembering his dependence on his Maker than modern man surrounded by the marvels and complications of scientific discovery. The superficial evidences are all against modern man remembering his creaturehood. The works of creation are now called 'raw material' and, as far back as a man can see, everything is man-made.

Vaguely, intermittently, the notion of creaturehood is accepted all round. But the notion is kept in its place. It is sensed that if this thought should ever become more than vague or intermittent in its action, it would be the greatest of disturbers. So steps are taken to keep it neutralised. Temptations to think are fled from. Doors are sealed up in the mind. Certain regions only are put at the disposal of the reason and the imagination. Flight from the pursuing thought ends in the most amazing absurdities, the greatest being that in which a man will take shelter from the thought in religion itself. He will attach himself to some vague minister of some vague religion. The minister, remembering his obligations to the fugitive from reality, will manage to preserve somehow his status as a divine without calling attention to the conclusions that follow logically from being a creature.

For the general run of people it is more to the point to contemplate a sense of creaturehood which is by no means so fantastically suppressed as this. Even the not-so-good can see those who are much better fail, in so far as they fail, from an imperfect realization of the fact that they are creatures. And several sorts of Christians accept all the implications of the words, *creature*, and *serving*, but manage to reveal no hint at all of having anything like a creature "complex."

Due for special notice under this head is the 'superior' sort of Christian. In relation to God he has no trouble in acknowledging his creature status, but in relation to men he is not so successful. Sophistication gone wrong is the cause of his trouble.

Things get out of focus for him. He develops a magnified vision of those who might be described as bad advertisements for religion, because they happen to be too fussy or too mechanical in their practice of it. The unintelligent and the over-obvious are an affliction to his spirit. He winces at the vigorous mixing of illiteracy and devotion. The trouble may have begun with his liver but in the end his normal vision is impaired and all things confirm him in his exclusiveness. Preachers with more zeal than parts become such an obsession for him that he hardly notices those others who are beyond his reproach. His eye is trained on the inept ones, and he spends his time adding up the clichés, the platitudes, the pointless superlatives.

Things of prize to the eyes of the angels are but futile to the eye of the superior Christian. He notes the unintelligent absorption with which some of the uncultivated read their prayerbook and wonders how many of them know the meaning of *vouchsafe*. But he wonders too much for his own good. He has gradually slipped out of his true place in the scheme of things. He no longer knows what is really important. He is even spiritually disfigured, being humble, so to say, in only one direction. He needs to take centre again, and the readiest way for him is to reflect seriously on what it means to be a creature.

VII

On being Sincere

WE PROBABLY HAVE DECIDED, or have taken it for granted, that we are truthful. We are able to sit back at ease while a dissertation on lying is spoken. The liar, as a human phenomenon, hardly interests us, for we are really far removed from him. We hear, without feeling, the philosophic examination of untruthfulness. We accept the fact that the liar is the most efficient undoer of right order. We come to realize the peculiar sort of unsatisfactoriness the liar has as a member of society; that he is and is not at the same time, that he has not *oneness,* is not integral, that we do not know where we are with him. Unmoved, rather, we observe the conclusion that universal untruthfulness would mean chaos.

Still not thoroughly interested in the liar—as we would be in the murderer, for instance—we note that his business is confusion and that he thus bears a close resemblance to the devil. We remember that Christ called the devil the Father of Lies—though we may not work out for ourselves the peculiar appositeness of this. With a sort of complacency we sit back and listen to the liar being presented as the diabolical deceiver he happens to be. He is a rare specimen. The sermon will be about the liar. Our withers remain unwrung. Truthfulness in ourselves we take for granted as before.

The sermon goes on to its close. The diabolical deceiver —the liar according to the book—is defeated out in the open. We are on the side of the preacher, and (which is still more comforting) the preacher is on our side. The sermon proves to be a vindication of us rather than an instruction. We are not the Horrible Example who has lived through the discourse and died in no uncertain manner in the peroration.

As far as it goes it is all very well. But a more marginal kind of meditation might have profited us more. Certain footnotes to the virtue of Sincerity, for instance, might have meant more to us.

It is significant that in our ordinary language we have more to say about people being 'sincere' or 'insincere', than about their being 'truthful' or 'untruthful.' We are not likely to dream of saying that this person or that is *living a lie*, but we may say—and we can mean a lot by it—that this person or that is a humbug.

The virtue of sincerity obviously lies in the correspondence between what we think and what we say. It is a fine point that we may not be *able* to achieve exact correspondence between our thought and our expression. In fact it is the inability to find the exact correlative that prevents many of us from being poets and artists. Such sincerity is however a condition of art rather than morality. A plain tale—enough for moral purposes—we can all tell if we will.

There is a grade of untruthfulness which in the wear and tear of life seems to have become inevitable, and to have attained to inculpability. (Recognised conventions like 'not at home' or 'not guilty' are not here meant). The fault is one that derives from a forgetfulness of responsibility, from a notion, it may be, that strict correspondence between the internal image and the outward expression is dispensed from, now and then, on the grounds that the strain of forever bringing it about is greater than can be borne. To ourselves, when we practise this particular style, it can look like an effort to contribute to the smooth working of life in general, whereas it is mostly a securing of smoothness for our particular selves.

Neither is this avoidance of the obligation of truth to be excused as a part of our tactfulness. Tact, after all, is skill in circumspection and anticipation. It secures that smoothness in conversation and affairs which is *due*, but tact does not mean smoothness at the expense of truth. A tactful woman will get through an awkward moment without telling her friend that she considers her (the friend's) new dress to be nearly un-sightly. An insincere woman, in the same circumstances, may even go so far as the word 'lovely'— though she will speak the word with a dying emphasis full of suspicion.

A lively, though not insidious, form of insincerity is a flair for exaggeration. Only the very perfect, the infinitesimal few, are quite free from it. Once or twice in our whole lifetime we may be privileged to be present when one of these, the elect, announces some piece of sensational news, or tells of a really amazing experience he has had, in a restrained economical fashion, tells it in the thoroughly satisfactory manner of a true transmitter, without adding one iota for effect, without evincing any wish to repeat it, showing, in fact, a reluctance to do so. And he does all this without affectation—for many will do the like but do it in such a way that we know their restraint is artifice, and even a trap to delude us into asking them to tell it again.

Amazement sits on all of us as we turn to the narrator whose story is sensational and whose way of telling it is so free from the deceptions of exaggeration. Our wonder is that he can remain so quiet with such a thing to tell. That he can so completely neglect this opportunity of taking the centre of the stage causes in us an amazement rivalling that which we experience at the story itself.

They, whose conversation is notorious for its incessant

exaggeration, set us a problem in computation rather than mislead us. All the time while they are narrating we are busy, like accountants, calculating and discounting. Or, to change the metaphor, these speak a different language, and we, through practice, have become expert in translating it.

Comparatively unimportant, because freakish and few, are those whose mechanism for externalising the concept in their minds seems to be permanently impaired. It is as if their minds were holding the images inverted as the eye's retina does, and they, through an imperfection in the apparatus of expression, delivered them still inverted. To the conversation of these we become not merely translators but decipherers. We listen to them with a mechanical caution, searching their speech for the fantasies caused by the defective apparatus, as we check a printer's proofs for misprints, and imputing not much more culpability to the speakers than we do to the printer.

Deserving of a classification to themselves are persons whose conversation is characterised by excessive assent. These rush to agreement with us. Often they go well before their cue and are expressing agreement before we have struck the verb, and before they can possibly know what we are going to say. If their speed should have misled them, it is no strain on them to switch again from 'yes' to 'no.' Nor are these to be confused with what the Americans call the 'Yes man.' Unlike 'Yes men' they retain their independence of mind, though in a state of suspension, and as likely as not will be peculiarly angular, difficult, and uncompromising when they are not making a point of being smooth. With these we have definitely come to the reprehensible. For their way, even if it be designed to contribute to easy and obliging ways in conversation, has the smoothness of insincerity.

The worst kind of smoothness is sycophancy. We do not become sycophantic overnight. The danger in this kind of meanness is that it can grow on us gradually. We have to keep remembering, if we wish to be safe, that the practice of the bowed head and the bent knee, even when becoming, or indeed a duty, does of its nature dispose us towards sycophancy. Excess of service is with difficulty kept from being subservience. The natural tendency is to speak a prince fair, and though this is in no way reprehensible, the least extension of it will be flattery. Courtiers have always had a bad name for sincerity. The likelihood is that they have deserved a better name than they got, for to an eye but slightly hostile all deferring may seem to be fawning. And yet, it is plain that they whose calling gives them the entry into high places must do some extra praying and fasting to preserve their sincerity.

By a nice irony it was a courtier who announced the standard of perfection in this matter: "To thine own self be true, and it must follow as the night the day thou canst not then be false to any man." Judged by that standard something of the courtier will be found in us all—perhaps a good deal of the courtier, when we consider how seldom we come to court. There is a thought to linger after the laugh in that story of the man congratulating the newly-made bishop. "You're alright now, my lord," said he, "you'll never eat a bad dinner or hear the truth again."

The temptation, at court, is to improve on due deference and to hasten to say the agreeable thing in all seasons. In the ways of human nature, as they are beaten out, many a one fails in this virtue of respecting persons without being a 'respecter of persons.' Our nature is strongly tempted to flattery, because we know so well that hardly anyone at all is proof against it. If we have the right bait we can nearly catch the saint. As in other things, we are prone to salve our conscience about flattery by bringing to mind some outlandish display or exponent of the vice and acquitting ourselves because we never fall so low. Yet often, when we are conscious that we are flattering a little (but only a little, we would say), we are differing only by a certain number of degrees from the obvious and disgusting type of flatterer. What difference there is lies mostly in technique.

The insincerity of others is palpable to us. We wince at it and are amazed by its grosser forms in the way that we are amazed by a monstrosity in the physical order. We hold our breath while a fellow—one of ourselves—breaks the code and presents the compliment that is too big for the occasion. We know, and the fellow knows, that this is not good enough. Right order is outraged. For a moment there is silence, while the one who is flattered adjusts his personality to the reception of the gross compliment. In silence we wait, as if out of the unseen we were expecting some protest to sound or some retribution to descend upon the head of the flatterer. We hold our breath while he gets away with it.

We keep a withering scorn for all who crook the pregnant hinges of the knee that profit may come of it. And our indignation blinds us. Thus, blind, we do not see that avoidance of such extremes is not the virtue of sincerity. We do not see the extent to which our own best efforts at being true to ourselves are modified. We like to make the most of conventions in order to free ourselves from the inconvenience of candour; and to make the most of conventions is dangerously like making too much of them. If we have not felt some strain now and then, and felt friction instead of smoothness, we may be sure we have not undergone fairly the ordeal of being true. The proverbial association of courage and convictions is significant.

An overdose of sincerity can be trying and troublesome. But, as it is so much the rarer fault, the first tendency is to welcome it as a contrast. Because of a degree of recklessness that goes with it, it makes an appeal to the heart. One is tempted to grant a full pardon on the head of it. In life, as in fiction, characters are redeemed by their hatred of sham. They win their way to the heart because they know not *seems*, and become heroes and heroines in tragedy because they avoid the subjunctive mood. Their protest against the flattery and smoothness of others often carries them on to stubbornness and truculence. Though an imperfection it wins sympathy, because it represents, above all things, a will to fight deception. It is out of the control of judgment, but it began nobly.

At the spectacle of flattery making a profit on the credulity of others, even mild and gentle folk have flared up and lost their heads. From hating the flatterers they have begun to despise the flattered, even when the flattered were those whom they loved. In the heat of the moment they have expressed some of their contempt. The friends have misinterpreted the source of that contempt and the knives have remained drawn. Before Lear, and since, many have been made foolish by flattery. And honest men have continued to side with the uncompromising forces of candour and have paid the penalty of coming between the dragon and his wrath. Honesty has fought itself to pieces and flattery has been left in possession of the field.

For excessive candour may pull down the house and in its recklessness throw victory to the enemy. But these things are lost sight of by those whose dominant passion is for flying at deceit. Their gorge rises at the sound of insincerity. Not for worlds, and not for their dearest friends, will they heave the heart into the mouth to speak what it does not mean. They have espoused so good a cause that they seem to us all nobility. Yet their weakness is apparent.

They are aware of their virtue before we are and are already putting too much emphasis on it. They are tempted into being proud of their candour. They are conscious of having the reputation of being outspoken people and begin to spoil it by showing an anxiety to live up to this reputation.

Perfection, as ever with the virtues, is in keeping a balance. While the insincere man or woman is completely unsatisfactory, the one bent on living up to a reputation for straightforwardness is not entirely desirable either. It is a significant thing that amongst all those who do nothing to deceive us we reserve the title of 'sincere' for only a few. Our first and distinguishing praise of these few is that they are 'sincere' men. Sincerity is in some special way an ornament of their being. In them it is something transcending truthfulness. They are more finely distinguished than others whom we know as 'very candid.' That which distinguishes them is like an ensemble of virtues. They are the thoroughly satisfactory speakers and listeners. Their good faith shines through them. We are never remotely troubled by a thought that we do not know where we are with them. Their quality is transparency, but not the sort that prevents subtlety. While their transparency in no way diminishes or makes less interesting the sort of mystery that goes with individuality, it secures us from being puzzled or irritated by another kind of complexity that is no perfection of personality. The satisfactoriness we find in them attaches to their silences as well as to their words; it is in tones and gestures and actions.

It is easier to describe them negatively than positively. They are not daring in their truthfulness, but they are certainly fearless. They are free from every suspicion of that secretiveness which is due to excessive caution and playing safe. They avoid the use of blunt speech as a device for showing character. They have a quiet kind of fame in their world, resting on a silent but universal acceptance of their reliability. They are finer people than those who make a kind of doubly favourable impression on us because we discover in the end that they are so much better than their word—finer too than those others who win us so completely—retrospectively—when we have made the discovery that their bark is so much worse than their bite.

The sincere have a bark that is the equal of their bite, but they are distinguished by neither. Their way has no drama in it, so that they remain unadvertised. It is only by reflection and casting about we come to realise that it is they who are the really valuable ones amongst our acquaintances. Motivated by an absolute sincerity, their style, like all good style, is inconspicuous and restrained: it does nothing for effect, it shrinks from show, it bides its time for ever.

VIII

On being Materialistic

To be free of all that is called *being materialistic* would be something like being a pure spirit with the use of a body. It would be a state of unmixed idealism. About such idealism there is a ruthless logic and incessant energy. Considerable inconveniences will arise if we have such a disturbing force within us. We begin to anticipate and evade these inconveniences in a way almost imperceptible to ourselves. Without seeming to do anything about it, we do in fact acquire a technique of protection that works automatically. One way or another we keep short of the consequences—the full consequences—of our beliefs. The idealist, when he happens, shows like a portent amongst us. He is the comet troubling our sky. Admiration of him is given with a sort of understanding that there shall follow no obligation to imitate.

The safety-first instinct of all of us whose sails are never to the tempest given has subtle ways of justifying itself. Some of these ways are much open to suspicion. One way is to assume our own standard as the right one and turn the idealist into a freak. The question is outrageously begged. The idealist, we say, is not 'practical.' With some overstress on the ways in which he differs from us he can easily be made to look quite funny. The funnier we make him look the more we are at ease in pursuing our own lower flight. If we put a disproportionate emphasis on his streak of idealism, the man with but one streak can be made to look absurd. We turn him into Don Quixote tilting at windmills. Sometimes the very circumstances help us to make a caricature of idealism, as when, for instance, Shelley, after having professed himself atheist, came to Ireland to help on the cause of Catholic Emancipation.

Not experiencing the fiery restlessness of idealism we make no such swift and unexpected journeys. We keep our place in the crowd. We are the crowd.

Far be it from me to censure us. But the contemplation of what we are not is a help to the realization of what we are. Other instances of idealism than the one just mentioned might be preferred—the idealism of saints for example. It is a point however that we may not be able to see the idealism of the saints so clearly as we see the idealism of Shelley. For even with the greatest saints we have much in common. We see them from the inside. Their cause is ours, and in part their idealism. The sensational sort of thing it is to follow an idea or devotion wherever it may lead, may strike our minds with more force when we picture Shelley, the professed enemy of the Christian religion standing in the streets of Dublin to distribute his pamphlet in support of Catholic Emancipation out of devotion to liberty in the abstract.

But the struggle of so many of us is not to keep breathlessly up with the implications of visions forever flaming before us. Ours is the plain tale. Our struggle—and it is fought at anything but a hectic pace—is against that most innocuous-seeming materialism, which is no more than the sum of our immediate comforts, and which so often succeeds in coming to terms with our souls for just this one more time. Gradually we perfect a fairly reliable mechanism for following what we call a 'middle course.' Conscientiously we submit this mechanism to our own inspection from time to time. From time to time, too, we go one better than the mechanism and give a flash or two of idealism. We feel the humbler and the better for it. And that in the main is us, the bulk of us.

To observe the idealist as a phenomenon, to study the quality and intensity of his devotion—and this we can do without attention to the *cause* of it—is an exercise that will do us good. It will do us good to reflect that, as often as the idealist marched out from beside us in the ranks of this cause or that and we stayed behind, we accepted the alternative, which is to be men of compromise—not dishonourable compromise but an acknowledgment that we were prepared to be something less than we were capable of being.

The thing of greatest moment remaining to us in our chosen state is that we be faithful to the compromise, to that line we have drawn above the essential commandments but below the counsels of perfection. At the end of our lives the story of the mass of us will be that we lived well our compromise, with one foot in each world. To have no higher aim than this is a thing repugnant to good sense—a fact clear enough, even before those trained in spirituality warn us. We cannot keep our level between the highest idealism and the lowest materialism without new efforts. But the efforts somehow get modified to suit our middle course.

The fact of living in both worlds together gives the advantage to this one. Each new move in the service of God pre-supposes a corresponding disengagement from Mammon. Mammon, who controls the forces of materialism, has his advertisements everywhere. Like all good advertisers he grows on people, until ideas, which they think to be their own, are really his. We often deceive ourselves, no doubt, when we further whittle down our compromise by thinking that we have received a fuller visitation of common sense.

These things may seem less like platitudes if we give them the form of a contemporary parable, and make materialism

contend with idealism on a quiet afternoon in the lounge of
a fashionable hotel. The contention is framed in the leisurely
conversation of two women. It is hardly conversation, for
one of the women has got into the mood for talking about
herself and her family, and the other is sitting back content
to listen. Their acquaintance is based on nothing more than
that their husbands have gone golfing together. As not un-
usually happens in such cases, the chance acquaintance re-
ceives a fuller revelation than do people nearer home.

The woman passes on from her daughters to her sons.
There are two. One of them is studying medicine; he will be
qualified next year. She lingers over this fact and yet makes
some pretence of not doing so—the affectation of uncon-
cern making it more plain that her heart is in this. Yet the
other son is her favourite. She checks herself from anything
like boasting about him, but it is plain that she could keep
talking of him for ever. This one is studying for the priest-
hood.

She holds that information back until she has hinted his
praises. Then she gives it with the air of one who announces
an anti-climax. She accompanies the announcement with a
gesture of resignation that has more of practice than spon-
taneity in it. Her resignation is of a negative kind, a sort of
passive acceptance of that which is incomprehensible as well
as inevitable. The satisfaction felt in the medical career is
missing here. She waits for the other woman to take up,
perhaps, the note of disappointment which she has insin-
uated more than expressed. For one reason or another the
other woman does not. But neither does the second woman
express any enthusiasm, and a meaningful silence falls
between them. The woman goes on with her story. She
keeps that slight tone of disappointment about her favourite
son. There is no trace of bitterness in her tone, no suggestion
of anything like ungodliness. The most there is is a quiet

sadness, as at the realization that a dream would never be fulfilled.

In such everyday scenes, in ways scarcely perceived, the compromise between materialism and idealism weakens in its wonted way towards materialism. The atmosphere in which the woman is speaking is at a high degree of secularization. It is holiday time, the comfortable lounge shuts out every single discomfort, her clothes are good, her husband is rich, she has a consciousness of great possessions, there is the satisfactory feel of good-living. It is against that background, too, that she sees her son with his black clothes and his breviary and his loneliness, a figure of contradiction.

An unfeeling zealot would not take long in opening her eyes to the inconsistency of being a Christian and thinking as she does. He would come straight and painfully to the point and ask her what was the purpose and end of life. And she, being a Christian, should have to answer in the words of the catechism and thus reveal to herself the folly to which she has now just come. The zealot might plunge her into Scripture and put her to shame by recalling the mother of the Machabees.

But such abrupt and unfeeling treatment may not in the long run be the best. The eyes must be gradually opened to this everyday materialism, which clings so closely to our thoughts and actions that it becomes part of us. Our motives are mixed by it, which is to say we hardly know where the good ends in us and the not-so-good begins. We even take our materialism to church with us. It is something we must be made to see in ourselves and persuaded out of. And no sooner have we by vigilance freed ourselves from materialism at one point than we have to be ready to begin against it at a score of other points. And so on, rather ad infinitum.

Nor is the case of the woman who is saddened because her

son has a vocation to the Church as simple in actual life as it may appear on the page. She suffers from spiritual short-sightedness, but she still gets down to her prayers. She is well aware that she cannot serve God and Mammon. She has very definitely elected to serve God and believes that she has the right view about Mammon. In short, she would be amazed that anyone should think of calling her a material-istic woman.

IX

On being Important

THE REFLECTIVE PERSON CAN SEE this world variously. He can see it either as a very big concern or a very small one. At one time all is but toys. At another he can see a heaven in a wild flower, or be bounded in a nutshell and count himself a king of infinite space. He need not be a poet to see it so variously, though he will naturally give the better account of it if he is. The mad Lear tearing off his clothes in the hovel to be level with Edgar and his blanket has a true vision, for all his madness. Edgar is the warning to all pomp, he is 'the thing itself, unaccommodated man.' Hamlet, marvelling like the psalmist at the nobility of man's nature—in action how like an angel, in apprehension how like a god—has a true vision too. Wisdom knows that both visions are true and keeps playing one against the other. It is only the person afflicted with self-importance who tries to have a fixed unvarying estimate.

To relate the concept, 'important,' to the general scheme of things is a task of some delicacy. There is one obvious distinction to be made. Certain persons and things are rated 'important' by us because of some quality or excellence inherent in them. Other persons are important because by authoritative decree they have been raised to positions of prominence. The selection of these for their positions will, no doubt, be due to their inherent qualities; their qualities, however, need not necessarily be such as would have made them important of themselves. But however a person's importance shall have come about, it in no way 'belongs' to himself. It consists rather in the estimate of others about him. It is a mark upon him which is visible to them but not to him.

As soon as a man tries to see in himself what others rightly see in him he descends to self-importance. Even the greatest person must—can—never be more to himself than the same old three-and-fourpence. As soon as he tries to be, he ceases to be. Montaigne remarked on a physiological necessity that cannot be dissociated from sitting on the highest throne. The present age would rate it a rude remark, but it has in it a degree of disenchantment that cannot be expressed by a substitute expression.

Being 'important' to others and being simultaneously the same old three-and-fourpence to oneself is a feat of adjustment for which special marks will, no doubt, be added in the next life; for the thing has its special difficulties. Thus, the unimaginative who have not themselves the label of importance tend to have a deleterious effect on all those who have the label. Because of not having a proper sense of distinctions they impose a severe strain on holders of high office by always implicitly demanding of them that they shall look important and sound important—taking no account at all of what an intolerable strain that would impose. Should the unimaginative themselves happen to be raised to positions with the label of importance upon them, they are in imminent danger of transferring the label from the office to their particular selves.

The self-important person puts a strain on all who are higher in the scale than he, because it is bad for his importance if those above him do not live well up to theirs. So the self-important one sets an exaggerated value upon seriousness. It is his native air. He feels better in it, there is less danger of exposure. Instinctively he knows that as long as conversation is kept serious, even unto dulness, the impression of his importance will survive. Pathetically he clings to and studies solemnity. Solemnity is for some the right and natural style. But the self-important man has no option: he must be solemn or go to the wall. Readily he allies himself with other self-important persons, and each one draws strength and comfort from the dullness of the rest.

For all his purely neutral states of mind, as well as for those that in any sense justify it, the victim of self-importance favours the grave visage. His portentous air is not really caused by what is happening in his mind. Nothing may be happening there. The grave look is a fixed affair, a screen, a mask. Not until something equivalent to a signal is given that it is no longer essential, will he put aside the mightily concerned look. His pointless solemnity becomes so habitual and mechanical that he can remain unaffected by that quip of the cynic about men who look more thoughtful than it is possible for any man to be.

Seriousness being his device, all else is a mortal trial for the self-important one. Humour troubles him. He is always waiting for it to die out in a conversation. He wants to get back into the safer dullness. He is embarrassed by the speed of humour, he cannot keep pace with it. He would love to despise it, but is strangely afraid to. For humour keeps rising before him like a ghost. As an abstraction he feels bound to respect humour. He has theories about it. The new psychology has broken in upon his peace. He has learned that a sense of humour is necessary for the completeness of personality. So he tries to come to terms with humour. He does something about it. He brushes up his humour; but he will join any league to keep it in its place.

The self-important are largely to blame for those misconceptions of humour and its 'importance' which beset the present age. Being funny at regular intervals, or at stated times, for the sake of one's mental health is one of the most fantastic notions of modern times. Knowing a number of funny stories with a view to telling them at the 'proper time', or driving oneself on to a marked cheerfulness of manner all because it has just being pointed out in a recent lecture that the saints were never sad, or that Christianity is a cheerful religion—this is not the humour that saves us from the folly of self-importance. But it is the sort or concept of humour that the present age is inclined to make its speciality.

'Has he a sense of humour?' the successful old head of the firm will ask in grave and measured tones about the new aspirant to the board. He will ask it as if it were something that could be discovered by the stethoscope, and as if the continued success of the firm depended on the newcomer's ability to see the old men's jokes. 'He has a wonderful sense of humour' one girl will reveal to another about the man she is going to marry. And they will both express relief, as if the success of the forthcoming marriage were essentially bound up with the fact that the man laughs his head off at the exploits of the Marx Brothers—though neither of the girls can see what he is laughing at at all.

It will be, in a routine way, noted of aspirants to religious communities whether they have a sense of humour. It will be mentioned in the same tone as sound lungs. But it may be that, during the aspirant's period of training, his genuine sense of humour will be no help to him if it varies to any degree from the uncertain and unreliable humour of his superior. The chances are that the superior will then call on the word 'levity,' or unwisely endeavour to pretend that the humour of a thing depends on the hour of the day. If a sense of humour is really a sense of proportion, then it is not a thing to be ordered about or driven into the holes and corners of the day: it must be always included in the individual's normal and natural expression of himself, bound up as it essentially is with whatever of wisdom and humility he possesses.

People, in short, will not have the right ideas about 'importance' if they have not the right ideas about 'humour.' If they have not enough value for humour they will have too much value for importance. And humour does remain suspect. The entirely humourless people (who are so often in charge of things) try to make humour unpopular at all times by calling it 'levity'—a treacherous word. Some repress their natural humour, and change their natures for the worse, out of deference to influential individuals who do not approve of humour. For, despite proverbs about wise men relishing folly, there is a lot of life in the misconception that the man who speaks the fool's part must be a fool.

A person who makes a joke at an unexpected time will have to work very hard at seriousness for a long time afterwards, if he is to convince certain sorts of people that he is completely sane. Falstaff has had the better chance with many because Shakespeare proved he was no fool by writing *Hamlet*. He who is remarkable for self-importance has a better chance of 'getting on' than he who is remarkable for humour—even though the self-important man is about the biggest joke there is.

Those who, while being important—either by their qualities or by their appointment—never lose sight of the joke involved in their being important, are the hope of our fallen nature. They are the truly humble. They win universal respect, and more than respect. They antagonise nobody, they make the thought of rebellion ashamed of itself. The superior who is of this quality moves amongst those over whom he is placed with none of that affected deference which is so often but the sign of relaxed absolutism. From him you will experience none of those sudden interjections of a rough emphasis which so completely banish from the mind the pleasant thought that a man might be a superior without seeming to be. The consciousness of his unworthiness to be in charge of anybody but himself (which in him is not over-shrinking but the plainest common sense) has left in his mind an indelible mark in the normal and natural way that the vivid perception of any truth will. But no embarrassment results from this, no studied humilities, no cultivation of fantastic feelings of unworthiness such as could not possibly be all the time maintained. To him his case is a straight case. The ordinary condition of his mind is an acknowledgment of the fact that his 'importance' is both a reality and a joke—though for practical purposes the joke must from time to time be overlooked.

Abstracting for the moment from consideration of right and wrong, we can broadly speak of two *styles* that are discernible in all human conduct. The one might be described simply as the style that is in keeping with the next world; the other is certainly the style that does best in this. That he who shouts is heard, that a person is taken at his own valuation, that the better thing to do with one's limitations is to pretend that they are not there, these are some of the postulates of the style that does best in this world. It is the style of the self-important man and of all who begin to be like him. It is the style that gives the 'best returns.' Not many, it must be said, endanger their prospects of getting on by pointing out that 'importance' has a funny side to it, and that most manifestations of importance are misleading. It is one of the jokes that is likely not to get seen. The occasional blithe and humble people who make the joke have little reward beyond their fun—which in their wisdom they can foresee, and, no doubt, they consider it sufficient.

Their case is exceptional and clear. Our case, with our mixed motives, is more difficult and of more consequence to us. We may have to do a lot of close pondering before we arrive at any fair idea of how far we have allowed the style that does best in this world to overcome in us the style that is more in keeping with the next.

X

On being a Judge of Others

JUDGING PEOPLE—DECIDING absolutely about them, computing their essence, locking them up in a cell in our minds for a life sentence—this should be something altogether out of our province. We can never know enough to do it right. It is essentially the function of a higher being. Cosmically considered, one man passing judgment on another is fantastic. It is the last word in presumption.

As an expedient for the better ordering of society some men are named judges. They are expected to play to the best of their ability the rôle of being something more than men. Selected for his wisdom, a judge will know that he wears his wig because, in the long run, it is the lesser of two evils for society that someone should wear it.

Judges apart, man passing judgment on man is engaged in a most irrational activity. The commonness of the practice of judging others is traceable either to an impoverishment of the mind, or to a failure in the beginning to train the mind's activities and make it more selective. Badly controlled curiosity and the habit of judging go together. Many are not easy in mind until they have made final judgments on both their friends and their enemies, until they have placed and pigeon-holed them. They conjecture until they have said (if only to themselves) the last word on their acquaintances. This is not done from any unworthy motive; and often there will be no other fault in the business than its pointlessness.

It is done rather out of a spirit of misapplied science, as if there were something unfitting in having dealings and communications—however satisfactory they be—with people who have not been finally catalogued. The gift horse is always looked in the mouth. Cataloguing is the passion. An unsatisfactory label will be better than none. When Bill is the subject of conversation his acquaintance will not be contented with the particular aspects of Bill that are sufficient for the conversation. The acquaintance wants to be able to round things off. He wants to be able to make some conclusive gestures, to clear his throat with a hint of the finality to come and say, 'Now I'll tell you the sort of man Bill is.'

"The proper study of mankind is man" said the poet, with an odd use of the word, *proper*. That there is nothing so interesting as people all are agreed. They whose minds are well nourished and cultivated avoid the pointless superlative. So also, in speaking of people, they refer only to the particular aspects of them that are the concern of the conversation, and so—by a very sense of the fitness of things— avoid the pointless judgment. But they whose minds are inferior in quality quickly get interested in the superlative and the completed judgment. A figure of this will be found in the finality with which a schoolboy writing a 'character-sketch' will dispose of a complex character out of fiction. Expert commentators will conclude lengthy investigations without venturing near that final classification of the character which the schoolboy will conclude in a page and a half. (Incidentally it is the expert's tentativeness, and not the schoolboy's assurance, that contains the compliment to the creator of the character. For, in acknowledging himself baulked by the individualising mystery of the character the expert points to that which is the seal of humanity and the proof that this character from fiction is lifelike.)

But no character from a book defies analysis so completely as does the least remarkable of living men. And so we come round again to the peculiar futility involved in trying to judge and classify men. The heart of the mystery of even the most commonplace of mortals will not be plucked out. It is a wonder we do not more often and more quickly come to realise how vain is our judging. How often, after he has been finally put away in his pigeon-hole, does not this man or that undo our classification of him by saying or doing something that we 'never dreamed' he would or could do.

We like to think the classifications we have made are sound and that others will agree with them. But, instead, we are ever finding that A (say), who is a man after our own heart, can only see B in a light very different from that in which we see him. And still we stick to the old futile game of general-judging and miss so much. Partly because of it we miss the thrill of the dazzling differences of creation. We are like people at a play who might spend all the time looking at the programme.

Those who fancy themselves to have a talent out of the ordinary for observing their neighbours eventually come to making too much of the talent. They begin to use it for entertainment. To prove how apt they are they take frequent examples. A tone of unmistakable sagacity is used and a claim to a sixth sense is implied. They seem to speak out of the depths of a hidden wisdom. The sixth sense is more often a detector of imperfection than of excellence. But as the 'talent' all the time looks like a talent, the possessor deems that the possession of it justifies its use.

This is a deceptive fault because one can be guilty of it while appearing to do no more than entertain a friend and fill in a dull period, especially if the friend is dull and almost impossible to entertain with any other kind of conversation. A worse aspect of the folly of turning conversation into final pronouncements on people is that it is morally impossible to revoke unfavourable judgments. To set out deliberately to publish another's praises (having previously concerned oneself with dispraise) is a sort of enterprise with something distinctly unreal and quixotic about it. To do it with any success requires far more skill than is required for the publication of something that is defaming. Praise is not so entertaining as scandal, and speaking praise has not so disinterested a ring as defamation.

Meantime God offers us a reward for not judging—for not taking the word out of His own mouth. The reward for being merciful in our opinion is that we shall experience the merciful silence of God when our own case is heard. We shall not, however, qualify for that reward by merely knowing about it. It is not enough to say of our neighbour, "We'll leave him to God" after we have first pretty well taken him to pieces.

XI

On being a Zealous Man

IT IS A RATHER COMMON MISTAKE with us (when we are discussing things of the spirit) to limit the word, *zeal*, too much. We reserve it for certain sorts of people more than we should. When someone says of a clergyman that he is a 'zealous man' we understand by it only one kind of man. This is the man who is formidable in his vocation, the man who is above all else distinguished by *action*, who in some unmistakable way is energetic to renew the face of the land, whose good works stand there—in stone frequently—for us all to see.

The formula is not comprehensive enough. There is the obvious omission in it—nearly too obvious for recording—of the person who effects a lot and yet somehow contrives to leave the impression that he has not done so much, or that the things done have been done by somebody else. The idea of so covering up his activities may be due to his peculiar temperament, to some unusual strain of fastidiousness, even to a sort of inverted pride. His charitable deeds may have been rather elaborately schemed in a certain way in order to leave no clues, and this be done because he finds a kind of innocent fun in doing it so. For one reason or another the many may fail in their observation of him. To those with better perception he is a clear case of the zealous man.

But a person might also be zealous and leave behind him no trail of effectuality even for the discerning. There is the one who burns inwardly with the fires of zeal, but shrinks from being a 'man of action.' His appearances in public are reduced a little below what is commonly regarded as the minimum. From being tentative in style he gets the name of being a slow mover. Though not interpreted as such, it may be his study of not giving offence that will be the part explanation of his restrained style. If he is a clergyman the popular impression of him will be that he is retiring and bookish—though much more of his reading than anyone thinks may be going to the preparation of his sermons. The sermons may end by going over the heads of the people. His worst enemy would not say that he is without zeal, but no one refers to him as a 'zealous man.'

It is the people whose zeal ends in *activities* who are in greatest danger from the excess of the virtue. They have ever at hand an external measure of their zeal, and, in the way of nature, they are in danger of keeping their eye too much upon the measure. Thus comes about one of the most easily discernible failures under the heading of zeal—the person who builds up everything except himself. Of more general interest—because more numerous—are the less obvious strayings from perfection. In all cases the trouble is due to a substitution of one's own glory for the glory of the cause one began by serving with considerable detachment. And this substitution may be done in the throes of a kind of theoretic humility. From exulting in the success of the cause one may come to estimating that success in terms of one's own achievement.

Zeal of this kind wears down humility. Those in high places can only survive in their first innocence by constantly inoculating themselves against it. Those who are given spiritual charge over others stand in the greatest danger of any, for the reason that spiritual charge is absolute in the way that no temporal charge is. The person given a spiritual charge of others will—presuming he is at all normal—begin with a thorough feeling of his unworthiness, of his unfitness and possibly (though this is not necessary to true humility) with the conviction that others he knew were far better fitted for the office than he. At the beginning he feels that he is standing out in the open, exposed too much to view, much embarrassed, a little helpless. Bending under the new weight of responsibility he looks even a pathetic figure.

The most profitable self-examination for such a one must naturally be to observe when and how any change comes in this first 'attitude' of his to his office, and, if a change has come, to note in how far it is due to *zeal*. Should the worst happen to him he will be found to have passed through various stages of belief in himself, marking a gradual deterioration from the days of his first distrust. The first stage will be simply a loss of his original distrust of himself. The thought will supervene that he is not, after all, so unsuited to this office as he had at first feared.

The second state is that in which he comes to thinking that there are, after all, good reasons why none of the others would—in the circumstances, etc.—have filled the office more successfully than he. Nor will he deem himself to be any less humble a man than when he first came to office. He will probably still have the same interest in the virtue of humility that he had at the beginning. But he now is prone to judge himself by different standards. Unconsciously he is measuring his success, and is influenced by it as a personal possession. The last extremity for him will be the belief that, after all, no man could have filled the office as well as he.

Though a part-time humility must appear highly fantastic in the view of Heaven, the absurdity of the spectacle is so well hidden from us mortals that many of us carry it off with not even a trace of affectation. A zealous person in high (or comparatively high) office is liable to it. Ordinary and rather trifling acts, which in a person of lowly state would be no more than mere acts of politeness, will begin to look like a significant expression of humility when they are the acts of one in high estate. Indiscriminate amazement at these manifestations by the simple people causes, eventually, a sort of permanent distortion. The unthinking will be heard exclaiming that some great man is wonderfully approachable—and indeed he may very well be—but the only proof they offer is that he has said 'good-morning' to them rather sweetly. Being human, the person in high office is prone to play a little with this device for producing humble actions. And he will be tempted to go out of his way to perform certain more unexpected actions of lowliness in order to secure the effect of a veritable fireworks of humility.

When we observe closely, and continue to observe, we cannot help being struck by the ease with which those in exalted places come to be commended for being unassuming. The popular misconception seems to be based on an assumption that the exalted ones have a right not to be. The fact is that they can so much more easily afford to be unassuming. An important test of their humility comes when their zeal is operative, when they are set for action. To express themselves in their office with zeal and at the same time remain humble, unassuming, approachable—this is the perfect union of forces.

Unless he keeps his humility tightly wrapped about him when his zeal is up, a person of high estate may be carried away and never get back to the place which he should never have left. Without the control of humility on his zeal what, for instance, will the honest failure of those under him look like? How easily the fair and normal expression of their independence (if it happens not to fit in with his particular recurrence of zeal) may seem to him opposition! Aware of his reputation for zeal (and it is very difficult for a zealous man not to be), thinking of himself, not merely as an instrument of God, but-as-an-instrument-of-God-destined-to-get-certain-results, he will be without the advantages of reflection which humility would offer in the face of opposition. He will be in real danger of the calamitous conclusion that opposition is an obstacle set to try him, that the more he is opposed the more it is a sign that God is with him. And if the worst comes to the worst he will call it martyrdom.

Begin where we will, we always find ourselves back at the same conclusion that success in the spiritual life is a matter of balancing, that virtue stands in the middle, that Prudence is the mother of all the virtues. Thus, the more zeal a man has the more humility he requires. Where zeal burns strong, a person is in a very real sense playing with fire. Never is the zealous man in more danger, for himself and for his cause, than when he runs into opposition. It is a challenge; and it is the self in him that jumps out to meet it. True Son of Thunder, he would then call down fire, and would want to call it holy fire.

The zealot can undo much good, for want of tempering his zeal; and, in addition, he does harm by supplying a text to those who are always ready to do nothing. Ungifted with fine sensitiveness—as he commonly is—the hour seems always propitious to the zealot. His imprudent insistence antagonises those who remember that the admonition, 'Do not cast your pearls before swine,' is directed against mis-placed activity and that neither pearls nor swine are necessary for its fulfilment. "Above all, gentlemen, no zeal" was Talleyrand's advice to his secretaries. It was shrewdness intended for this life, but it will serve well for the next. Many a good cause fails because its advocates and promoters distinguish themselves by neglect of that advice.

There were some of His disciples, who, out of zeal for Him and for His cause (and perhaps a little for themselves) would have Christ go here instead of there and, in general, quicken His pace, forgetting, as the zealous man is prone to forget, the wisdom of doing things in God's good time.

XII

On being a Snob

WHILE IT IS PECULIARLY EASY to see a fair element—or even much more than that—of snobbery in others, it is only with the very greatest reluctance we will admit that there is any of it in ourselves. Snobbery is the sin of others. Again, while it is commonly but a light fault, it is unfailingly given a hard judgment—this, no doubt, because it is the sin of others. Instances of snobbery in a really ugly form are rare; in its venial forms it is universal. There comes a point when the fault is scarcely perceptible at all, when only a trained psychologist will not mistake it for an accomplishment or an art form.

In short, the human mind has got badly twisted in respect of snobbery. In so far as it is a weakness it is the most common of weaknesses. But the word has a rather fearful aspect, so that a man will try to keep it from him at any price. The simple fault is exaggerated out of all proportion. Its comparative innocence, its childishness, is not attended to.

We are quite accustomed to speaking of justifiable ambition, of laudable ambition. We deem it a good thing. We commend the man who seeks to better himself—we heartily commend him while he is about it and before he has actually done so. But as soon as it is apparent that he has definitely succeeded, we are tempted to call back our commendations and think the successful one a snob. And the greater the measure of his success the more evidence we *seem* to have that he is a snob.

If we put ourselves in the place of the successful man, we begin to see the case differently—more leniently. Bettering ourselves—our policy of justifiable ambition—implies first of all belief in our ability to succeed. It implies an active hope, a steady looking upwards. It implies too—as part of our plan for getting on—that we will tend to see ourselves a little in advance of where we have got to, rather than a little short of it. (This is only good tactics). We then carry our heads a shade or two higher than there is present warrant for. What a temptation for all the others to think that we are putting on airs, that we are snobs. Are we? Perhaps we deliberately decide to look more like tuppence-half-penny than tuppence, as part of a general scheme for one day arriving at being a genuine threepence. Is this snobbery according to the book? Or is something to be allowed for extenuating circumstances?

Our charge against some has been that they 'loved a lord.' But, if we are really honest about it, and observe ourselves fairly, we shall have to admit that we all do. Protesting does not save us. Those who protest too much, and those who are ever ready to hint at social-climbing as a weakness in others, only reveal how much their own tendency is in that direction. Nor must we fail to observe the case of the frustrated snob who through unfavourable circumstances or lack of aptitude has not become the sort of social success that his nature prompts him to, and who tries to compensate his feelings by reading his own weakness into others. This man's indignation is founded entirely on his own snobbery, and he is wearisome because he takes snobbery much too seriously.

Those saints most renowned for detachment may have rid themselves of this last infirmity of the mind, but not many others have done it. How few they are who do not feel *some* satisfaction at being treated (though it is only by mistake) as if they were size seven or eight in the scheme of things, when really they are but size six, or five.

How many, who are themselves given to wholesale denunciation of snobbery in others, will lose no opportunity —will even patiently make opportunity—to hint that they or some member of their family has connection or association with people of account. The connection may be very tenuous but it gives satisfaction. May not the religious who has detached himself from the world yet hear with satisfaction in his cloister that his family has bought another farm or a bigger house? That very man who all his life has made a point of not being thought a snob may succumb at his father's funeral by experiencing (and expressing) a keener satisfaction at seeing the Smith-Browns there than he experiences at seeing either the Smiths or the Browns.

The person who says there is nothing of snobbery in him is making a claim almost intolerable to nature. You will be able, if you look very closely, to detect a sprig of snobbery offshooting from the most charming and natural humility. Nor will you, unless you are a curmudgeonly fellow, experience much distress at it. If your ear is sharp you will detect overtones of snobbery in the conversation of the elect.

With what a subtle tone of artless triumphing (even while he whispers in the low accents of self-effacement) a humble man will draw attention—in passing—to the fact that the people to whom he is referring (and whose identification is not necessary to his communication) are the So and So's of Such and Such—important, significant people. How the head of a school will purr inwardly with satisfaction to hear one parent tell another in his presence that the school produces a "nice type" of boy, even though the head knows that the parent speaking the compliment is not well qualified to judge and has no more reliable measure of these things than the size of the fees.

Only the cruder and more vulgar forms of snobbery are reprehensible, and we must be careful not to take our measure of what is snobbery from the frustrated snob who is always so ready to give it. We must only smile at the head of the school purring inwardly from insufficient causes, and smile, too, at the parent who wrecks the conversation in order to tell us that his son is at a school, the name of which is intended to impress us—though in this case the effort to smile takes more out of us. For all manifestations of snobbery, short of the crude, it is everyone's interest to plead a ready forgiveness.

We might go even farther and be prepared to make a case for much that is called snobbery. When all the jokes have been made against the vulgarity of the newly-rich, when due account has been taken of the fact that high thinking may be found along with plain living, it is still the fact of history that good style more usually goes with ample means and the bigger house. What is more likely, and indeed more pardonable, than that people should be tempted to bear themselves as if their means were more ample and their houses bigger than in fact they are.

A special sort of sympathy must be felt for those who experience a sudden rise of fortune. If they wish to escape completely the charge of snobbery they will have to act quite hypocritically. To be free of the more relentless judges they will now have to pretend to be poorer and of less account than they were. Grievous offence can now be given by a trifling gesture.

All this will have sounded so like a sermon that a short summary, by way of peroration, will hardly be unexpected. The summary is, that with the exception of the greater saints every man and woman is a snob of sorts. The fault is a very pardonable one except in the case of (a) those who will not admit that they are snobs, (b) those who express their snobbery crudely and vulgarly, and (c) those who are more attentive to the snobbery of others than they are to their own.

XIII

On thinking Oneself to Stand

A S A WISE MAN OF OUR DAY has put it, there is one point at which a man stands, several at which he falls. From much farther away comes the voice of Paul of Tarsus, saying, "Let him who thinketh himself to stand beware lest he fall." Perfection is a matter of balancing. Here is the special problem of The Good. And the better a person becomes the more this becomes his problem. It is hard to be good without having some inkling, some remote suspicion of it. Man's nature makes this the first stage in a temptation to approve of himself.

Self-consciousness is a sort of enemy. It is hard for us not to become observers of our own actions in such a way that they come to have a hypnotic effect on ourselves. We find this in the whole range of our activities, and not merely where there is question of acts that have a moral value. People who recite things in public will tell you that they are alright until they advert to the fact that they are remembering, and then they are in danger of breaking down. A man operating a complicated piece of machinery does it best when he does it absolutely mechanically. If he thinks about how he is doing it, he may not be able to do it at all. The golfer (whose game supplies so many apt illustrations for the spiritual life) knows it is fatal to be 'looking at himself playing.'

St. Paul's warning about not thinking ourselves to stand was not issued for exceptional cases, but for everyone—and he made sure to include himself. Obviously the warning has special point for the elite. The higher one has reached the more temptation there is to admire oneself and the greater must be the fall. Being perfect, or near it, is a breath-taking performance—it means balancing on a point. The acrobat will perform his first run of tricks with an easy and almost careless assurance. But when he comes to the climax of his act he seems to succeed only by a strange mingling of distrust and hope. The first simplicities have given place to complexity and intricacy. Keener calculation is required and a finer touch. That crowning performance to his act is achieved only by a series of the most tentatively done actions, each done by holding the breath, until the last, the perfecting touch, is added as if by a miracle of gentleness.

This last act of the acrobat may be as good an illustration of humility as we are likely to get. He succeeds by neither under-rating or over-rating himself. His estimate of himself is made up of fear and trust.

The man who is truly reflective cannot be anything but humble. There is nothing so logical as humility. And yet the logic of it is not forced upon us, because in the world it is so easy to 'get on' without either logic or humility. The 'style of the world' is not based upon reflection (beyond that degree which is absolutely necessary for 'getting on'). Everything that bears upon the senses encourages the man of five talents to feel superior to the man with four.

The 'style of the world' is very taking. To sit at the top of the table with sentiments (unaffected ones) appropriate for sitting at the bottom of it is not as easy as vice versa. Indeed when a place has been acquired at the top the temptation is to forget that there is a bottom. The Pharisees whose way Christ marked for disapproval went automatically to the top, lulled, no doubt from long practice, into the delusion that their right there depended on their merits.

While the humble will be exalted, it does not follow that

all who find themselves sitting at the bottom of the table in this life will find themselves at the top in the next. Everything depends on the dispositions with which the lowest as well as the highest seats are taken. A person may choose the bottom of the table because he thinks the company better there. In so far as this is humility it must be said to be its own reward. The good fortune of the man who sits in the lowest place and is told to go up higher is so attractive, and, on the face of it, so easily achieved that our imperfect nature is tempted to use the lowest place as a device. So, we may see a man take up his position at the bottom of the table, but with such overdone emphasis as to make it quite apparent that he is convinced his proper place is at the top. If nobody says 'Give this man place'—and unfortunately someone always does—he will not run the risk a second time.

The only person who adequately fills the lowest place is he who knows it is good enough for him. When he is bidden to take the highest place, he does not get any ideas about himself, but calmly realises that he is now out of his element. He does not get either frightened or subservient. He still has a mind appropriate for sitting in the lowest place and it would not cost him a thought to go back there. While others of more imperfect disposition will have measured out a score of intermediate degrees of honour and precedence between top and bottom, he will be worried about none and will be capable of confusing the top with the bottom. His serenity looks like unconsciousness and he has almost performed the miracle of being humble without knowing what humility is.

The humble man will be the first to admit that it is fitting to have front seats for those who hold high offices. If he is a holder of high office himself he will go and sit in a front seat with no more display of humility than he would have given in taking the most inconspicuous place. Personal feeling does not enter into it at all. He does not mistake the honour done to his office for any complimentary gesture to his own person or individual worth. The rules of precedence he respects, no matter where his own place be. He sees how useful the rules are for preventing confusion and saving time. He knows they represent a convention merely, and that they are not necessarily according to the only assessment of merits that will count in the end.

But about all this it never occurs to him to grow romantic or indignant. He can sit at the bottom of the table without wanting to start a revolution, as he can sit at the top without forgetting there is a bottom. The thought that there won't be enough room at the bottom of the table may occur to the cynic, but the humble man knows everyone has first claim there.

Our prejudices are great preventers of humility and balance. Our trouble will not be with those obvious prejudices which float often upon the surface of our conversation and must eventually be plainly seen even by ourselves. The real preventers of humility are our more ultimate prejudices, the ones that are never on the surface but are of the very contour of our minds and have the force of axioms with us.

Those deeper and ultimate prejudices will be found, for instance, amongst the assumptions—we find it hard to think of them as *assumptions*—which are lodged in our minds in favour of our own set or country. Nothing is more natural than that we should feel an undying affection for our origins. But it is easy to exceed the virtue of *pietas* and on this very matter become wanting in flexibility. No matter what our nation is—big one or small—we will (if we are humble people) have schooled ourselves into hearing with patience, and with profit, that not all our national characteristics are virtues. We have not the flexibility of humility until we can see and acknowledge the virtues as well as the vices of nations that may have injured us. Everyone can see the joke in: My country, right or wrong—when it is put like that. When the same joke is put in other terms, it frequently does not get seen. In all this field humility gets a singularly hard time from prejudice: true detachment in giving judgment as between our own nation and others is so rare as to be invariably suspect.

That self-praise is no recommendation is a saying due for extension to groups and countries. If a country's praise is to be spoken, it is better that it should be spoken from outside —or in Heaven, if the glory is not to be here. Most countries are given to thinking of themselves as standing highest in God's sight. All over the globe we find ourselves in 'God's own country.' The plurality of claimants is disillusioning, and the element of competition which enters in is notoriously bad for humility. Also, the presumption by any nation that it is the elect of God can only ill-fit it for seeing the merits of the others.

As we will be the better for being humble (which does not mean poor-spirited) in respect of our country, so too in respect of any group to which we happen to belong. Particularly is this true if it is a group for promoting ideas; and truest of all when it is a group for religious purposes.

If we are members of a religious order, it cannot be without danger to our humility and desired flexibility of judgment that we conclude that our order has been favoured above others. Loyalty to their order by individual members must be always a just cause for admiration of them in all outsiders. But the order must not take it too badly if an outsider should be temerarious enough to wonder why members of the order always happen to hold the views of the historic theologians of their order in opposition to the views of the historic theologians of other orders on open questions in theology. Touching, too, is that loyalty—though it does not quite escape our question—with which members of an order in their preaching will call exclusively on the saints of their own order to illustrate the virtues.

Again and again in the gospels we encounter the voice and gesture of provincialism and each time Christ reproves it. Nathaniel did not think much of anyone coming from Nazareth. Nazareth seeking its own fame, took the view that, if there were going to be miracles, it had a better claim to them than Capharnaum. The Nazarenes spoke their mind. And another Prophet was without honour in his own country, for Christ refused to bow to their provincialism. The woman at the well in Sichar thought that her own province, Samaria, was God's chosen ground; though—still provincial—she admitted that there was a view in favour of the neighbouring province. The time was coming, Christ told her, when it would be neither the one nor the other. The Galilean disciples must have swallowed hard over the brotherly-love parable on finding that the hero of it was a Samaritan. One can imagine a modern version of the same parable—with a different sort of foreigner substituted for the Samaritan—which would give offence in other countries.

The mother of the sons of Zebedee, lacking the centrality of view that comes from humility, sought a declaration of priority in favour of her own two sons. She was rebuked. Another woman in unrestrained admiration of Christ's preaching cried out: "Blessed is the womb that bore thee and the paps that gave thee suck." Though it was a cry from the heart and stirred memories, it was a distraction. Directing the minds of his hearers away from considerations of local or personal interest, however good, Christ restored the emphasis with: "Yea rather, blessed are they who hear the word of God and keep it."

Again and again Christ rebuked the racialism that is as

deadly as greed, the limiting nationalism, the provincial pre-judice. Salvation was 'from the Jews,' but everything was said and done by Him to make it clear that they should have no corner in it. Everything was said and done to disengage the minds of his disciples from false ideas of rights and preferences in respect of Himself and His kingdom, and to give them flexibility of mind about the Church He had come to found. Far above the local rivalries and far beyond the limits of whatever geography they knew went the words visioning the future: Many shall come from the East and the West . . .

XIV

On being Fair to Saint Peter

SYMPATHY IS DUE TO THE PREACHER as he ascends the pulpit faced with that first task of banishing distraction, of gripping the minds of the congregation. Forever the same audience and the same preacher—it is not so easy to be stimulating as the critics suppose. To catch their ear by a trick, to startle and draw them to him at the very first go by a lively paradox—the preacher must be at times tempted to something like that.

Arrived in the pulpit, he pauses for a quick survey of the scene before opening his mouth. He remarks that too passive, too submissive way of theirs. On the upturned countenances he sees the look of great expectancy, which does not altogether mislead him. For that look, he knows, is something of a mask, and underneath it they are telling themselves that they know very well what he is going to say. There is a sort of challenge in it. He is tempted to banish their irritating complacency. He could do it by going off on some totally unexpected line, by giving a new twist to the interpretation of a parable, for instance.

They all know so well what he is going to say about the Good Samaritan. They look reconciled, more than attentive, as he comes to point the moral of it.

He might fairly wake them up by denouncing this good Samaritan. He might shake his head at the Samaritan and say in withering tones: "How very like this Samaritan we are, you and I and all of us. We like the glory and the praise, but we do not like doing the work. We look for the credit and let the innkeeper do the work. Our charity costs us little."

That would do it—but at a cost. It would not get past the thoughtful ones. They would remember that the whole point of Christ's parable was that the Samaritan—and not the innkeeper—was the hero of it. Besides this is too obvious a piece of sensationalism. Such a liberty is seldom taken. But liberties of a lesser kind are taken, and not always by preachers who are, or feel, driven to such devices. The preacher who has fairly got his audience will try a little novelty for greater effect. The habit grows, and more and more preachers are drawn on to trying for that little additional liveliness in their discourses. The general intention is good—to make some incident in the Gospel more vivid for us, to make us more immediately aware of it. In the Gospel story there is some room for the imagination to work: but the trouble begins when the imagination takes more room than there is.

The silences in the Gospel are such as we do not like to hear speculated about except delicately and tactfully. Otherwise we feel a discomfort which can so very easily become acute. The blanks must be filled in by a tentative hand, a hand always ready to leave off.

We have heard it otherwise too often—a total account presented of the psychology of Peter, not a shred of mystery left to cover the infamy of Judas. In this bad style the way is to swing high or low in interpretation according to the immediate need of the preacher. In to-day's sermon it may suit to have the Apostles stupid and very insensitive fellows. In to-morrow's they may appear as the models of all good seminarians gathered round their Teacher, Christ, who may be presented to us as a modern Master of Novices.

No one gets a harder time than Saint Peter. There is an unusual convenience found in his story: he will illustrate such a variety of faults and failings. As if they were trading upon the belief that he was the sort of man who can take it well, preachers take the greatest liberties with him. When they have asked us to see ourselves as the lowest of the low, and at the same time want us to keep in mind that there is still hope for us, they are almost sure to say, 'Look at St. Peter.' In this there is, no doubt, an implied compliment to his humility. But still . . . And when there is question of the 'plain' man, in any of his shapes and forms, Saint Peter must appear. We have often felt heartily sorry for him. It is true that we think of Peter as a man in the category of the simple rather than the complex; but the simplest soul is entitled to have more complication of mind attributed to him than is allowed by many a preacher to the head of the Apostles.

Through being used so much as an illustration, Saint Peter has for many people got out of proper focus. The different aspects of his character have been consistently presented in such isolation from one another that we overlook the fact that he was a man in whose make-up the elements of strength and weakness were mixed in the normally mystifying way of human nature.

Peter believed in his loyalty to his Master, which is to say that he believed that in any circumstances or danger he would stand by his Master. While passing due censure on Peter for a too-indiscriminate belief in his own loyalty, we might—in a sort of fairness to him—reflect that the generality of men have a more unquestioning faith in their loyalties than in any other good quality which they believe themselves to possess. Those more given to introspection than St. Peter probably was will say that this is because feelings of loyalty and of pride lie very close together. But that is by the way.

Peter had one very good reason for believing in his loyalty. Physical courage came natural to him. A man knows when he is like that. Peter knew that if there was going to be a fight he could rely on himself. It is not fair to conclude—as is done—that Peter was a boastful man because he backed himself to remain loyal. It is more to the point to reflect that his loyalty was the only thing in himself that Peter ever was prepared to back. He failed as it happened. But his strength did in fact lie there; and he is not necessarily a boastful man who claims one virtue.

When he was warned and told to think twice, Peter would not. This was a bad business. If his failure consisted in a complete shutting of the mind to any persuasion, then it was that sort of stubborness which makes us want to kick men more than condemn them. His belief in his own powers of being loyal, his complete refusal to question them, might too have been traceable to his feeling—a happening in the sub-conscious rather than in the conscious mind—that he was made in such a way that he *could not* fail his Master. It would still be a fault and something requiring cure, but a failing with a sort of goodness in it. And in all this matter we, of course, owe it to St. Peter to recall that we have the advantage of him. He did not have any book with references to the 'presumption' of St. Peter in it.

It is much harder to excuse Peter's saying in the hearing of the other Apostles that he thought it not impossible that *they* might not stand the test. We may suppose that it was, in fact, a fair and well-based calculation of Peter's that he would be, at the very least, as good as any of the others if it came to a fight. To say it, as well as think it, was uncalled-for candour, the sort of thing that is not done.

"Let him who thinketh himself to stand beware lest he fall." Peter stood, but he did not beware. When he saw trouble coming he bought a sword and used it in spite of death. But before he entered the courtyard of the high priest he had been notably guilty of presumption and bad manners.

He still felt sure of his loyalty to his Master. From what we know of him he does not seem to us the style of man who found things out by reflection. Perhaps he was a better judge in other matters. This, for certain, was his blind spot. Here he had to learn a lot by experience. We are in all likelihood justified in thinking that if we had been in Peter's place we would have paid more attention than he did to the warning of Christ. That does not seem an extravagant claim on our part. The warning was very plain: *all* the sheep would be scattered. Imprudence (and who shall say how much of it was pride and how much loyalty?) gave the too swift answer for Peter: 'Except me, Lord.'

We feel we would have avoided that. And yet again it will be better for us not to record a wholesale victory over Peter. There is no parity at all between our states. We are reading it in a book. We are not there in the night with a sword at our side. We are not restless, apprehensive, excited as he was. We are not in the position of having failed in one trust (sleeping during the watch) and being doubly determined that we shall not fail again. We are not *tempted,* as he was, by the very circumstances of that hour, to protest too much.

And yet any man so sure of himself as Peter then was will not do. Imagine him getting away with it. How unfitted he would be for the work to come, how unfitted for Heaven. His story shows in an unmissable way the ontological necessity for *conversion*. He lived too close to his own defect. His weakness was too near his strength. It was never going to dawn on him. He had to be 'lessoned.' The cock-sureness had to go; he had to be changed into a Peter who, even in the protestation of his loyalty, would include that doubt of himself which a creature always must include because he is a creature.

He apparently had none of that imaginativeness that might have given him a hint beforehand of some such state of things as did actually come to pass after the arrest of Christ. In a confused way Peter thought in terms of heroics. Though he was told to sheathe his sword, yet there was mention of twelve legions of angels. Anything might happen yet. How entirely unprepared he was for that leisurely, humdrum, anticlimactical experience in the courtyard, where the gossip of the servants went on around the fire, and Peter became the subject of their talk merely because his presence there was unexpected and he served as well as anything else.

Just why Peter uttered the denials that he had been of the company of Christ is something we now can only guess at. Preachers, in their eagerness with a lesson for us, should not be so sure that they know. It may have been this that prompted him, or that. Perhaps he could not have sorted out the motive himself.

How far was fear a motive? That it was the only motive does not seem a good guess. It may have been that, in the air of unspectacular failure in which he saw everything from the time he entered the courtyard, he felt, for the first time since he became a disciple of Christ, that there was not after all much 'point' in it. It may have seemed like that to him. The old forces were still on top. He had left his fishing, but the world had not changed. The world was not going to change, nothing was. The dream was an unsubstantial dream. These unchanged faces lit by the light of the fire were the reality. It was he who was unreal under their insolent stare.

In that contracted, deflated mood, if someone had asked him was he one of Christ's men he might have hoped to get out easily by simply saying that he was not. He could even have begun to wish that he did not belong, even to see himself in the future as no longer belonging. Shame more than fear may have entered into him. And then when those around the fire guessed the lie and—in the merciless way of man—followed it up, he would not see himself exposed as a liar before them. The great thing, the immediate need now, was not to be defeated or shown up in the eyes of those men and women. The vehemence of Peter at this point, his swearing that he did not know Christ, sounds like that of a man whose mind is dominated for the moment by one idea only—that he won't be shown up. He sounds a Peter too bad to be true; and it looks as if they all saw through him.

There is not much point in our ever spending much time estimating the extent of Peter's guilt. We can learn the lesson that is there for us without taking on ourselves computations which are none of our business. Hence it is distressing to hear preachers using the word *Apostacy* here of Peter, and using it in such a literal way as indicates that they have classified it with sins 'specially reserved.' There is no use in their talking to us like men pretending that they were there—and only narrowly missed hearing St. Peter's confession.

What was that look which Christ gave to Peter, we wonder. We know what the effect of it on Peter was, but we know no more. Was it a look that reproached Peter with apostacy? Or was it a look that seemed not to delay over the fact of Peter's denial, but rather carried him back to the unheeded warning and taught him in a moment the lesson of humility necessary for his conversion? St. John, who alone of the four Evangelists, may have seen the look on Christ's face, says nothing of it. When Peter went out and wept bitterly how much was his mind occupied with the thought that he had denied his Master, and how much with the thought that he had set his own assurance above his Master's warning? One was effect and the other cause. Peter's conversion required the removal of the cause.

Certain lessons are made very plain for us out of Peter's story without our distorting it in any way. But many questions start up that none should pretend to know the answers to. St. Matthew reports: "Peter followed at a long distance to see the end." How much that *to see* leaves unanswered. In what frame of mind did Peter follow? Had he plan or aim as he entered the courtyard? Who knows? Did he know himself? Was it a sort of automatic action after the arrest of his Master? Was he *drawn* to the scene, as an imaginative writer might put it—and what precisely would the imaginative writer mean?

Our uneasiness, we repeat, is great when preachers or writers affect to be in no doubt about the answers to these questions, and go on to base moralizings on their dogmatisms. And the dogmatisms cancel one another out. The other Apostles will be blamed for their pusillanimity in running away when Christ was taken. But Peter will be blamed for following. Curiosity (unbridled) will be the fault attributed to him. He will be held up to us as an illustration of the dangers of curiosity. In Peter's case it will be said that curiosity led him amongst the enemies of God and his soul, that curiosity led him into the sin of Apostacy. The reading of the Gospel story (to suit this case) will be that Peter was not so much following his Master as seeking the company of the servants in the courtyard. From such an absurdity it is but one more stage to saying that he went there to warm himself.

Having it not only both ways, but every way, in interpretation is a questionable aid to preaching. The gaps and silences in the gospel narrative, the touches of mystery that will be mystery for ever, the inconsistencies that are the stamp of humanity on Peter and others, impress our minds more forcibly than guess-work pretending to be more.

On Thinking in the Heart

THE SPIRITUAL DESOLATION of a people who have forgotten God is something we have no difficulty in seeing. Their characteristic is mechanism, mechanical living. Everyone who sets about reforming them speaks of a 'change of heart' until the phrase is a cliché. Mechanism substituted for thought on such a large scale—in a whole people—we cannot miss seeing. But, on a smaller scale, in our single selves, there may be quite an unattractive mechanism that we are not conscious of at all.

"We see the majority of mankind going most often to definite ends, lower or higher ends, as their own instincts may determine; but the end may never be attained, and the means may not be quite the right means, great ends and little ones alike being, for the most part, distant, and the ways to them, in this world, somewhat vague. Meantime, to higher or lower ends, they move too often with something of a sad countenance, with hurried and ignoble gait, becoming unconsciously, something like thorns, in their anxiety to bear grapes; it being possible for people, in the pursuit of even great ends, to become themselves thin and impoverished in spirit . . ." This was not written in any treatise on religion or the spiritual life. But it can quite obviously be made to apply.

The proof that we are satisfied with what we have is that we are not on the look out for more. In a way this holds for things spiritual. How, for instance, do we feel about what we may call the element of *richness* in the Christian revelation? What is our personal appreciation of all the wonders that make it up? To what extent do we feel that we have been given into our hands more treasure than they can hold? Or is the life gone out of our formula for thanks from want of thought? How often does it happen to us—does it ever happen?—that we feel embarrassment at the number of these riches? Do we experience at the thought of them a sensation such as a keen reader experiences at standing in a vast library and seeing everywhere books that he has long wanted to read and, because of their number, will never succeed in reading?

To the man who has appreciation of it the barest outline of Christian revelation seems more than his mind can contain. He is hard pressed to make room or time for all that has happened in the church since the days of the Apostles. He is aware of such a multitude of reasons and incentives for perfection before 100 A.D., that he is really concerned to know how he can cope with all that has been added since that time. What is to be said of us, then, if we are for ever disposed to seek a new stimulant?

That, perhaps, is putting it too extremely and too crudely. But there is a sort of interest in a new 'way' which too plainly indicates that the old does not mean nearly enough to us, that our sense of proportion has got badly knocked about. The faith by which a Christian lived in Apostolic times is that by which a Christian should still live. This is a truism, but a truism to have in mind when we investigate how much and what kind of emphasis we place on things that were unknown to the Apostles. Let us put it like this. The Christians of Apostolic times were not without a sufficiency of spiritual props. Add to these the multitudinous ones of the intervening two thousand years. What is the result? Each individual must give his own answer. Our concern here is the general consideration of a characteristic weakness in our nature, namely that the multiplication of riches takes the edge off appreciation. There *could* be a tendency to take for granted, to undervalue. And that is the first sign of mechanism.

Mechanism means that our imagination has ceased to play its part. To be without imagination means—to take one instance—that we have, however unwittingly, slipped into a way of assuming that because we have given a name to a mystery and related it to other things in a scheme, we have thereby got nearer somehow to the heart of it. We are in some danger of being less impressed by the mystery because we have included it in a system—the human mind being especially susceptible to valuing too highly its own power of classification. Do we fall into a mechanical way of dealing in terms rather than in things and mistake our very readiness in the use of the terms for a closer association with the things they stand for, often times being not much more attentive to the terms' implications than men are attentive to the implications of the coins they give and take mechanically in exchange, seeming in the end to live by them and for them?

We do no wrong. Our good-will is not wanting. In fact, we may live very religiously, very conscientiously, though we are most of the time on the surface, far from the heart of things. It is rather that we go on missing the point. And as missing the point gets the same result for us—though it be more excusably—that a refusal to think in the heart gets, we must expect a desolation of the spirit to follow from it.

'I could be bounded in a nut-shell and count myself a king of infinite space' is the voice of reflection—a logical claim too, if there be 'sermons in stones.' To the infinite range of the mind's speculation add the range of the will's affections, shown negatively to us in a poet's rebuke: 'A primrose by the river's brim a yellow primrose was to him, and it was nothing more.' Add these together to find the extensive country of the contemplative man's mind. If from the contemplation of stones and primroses thoughts lead back to God—but there is no need to draw out the conclusion. Only it is wisdom not to forget that, when we have passed outside the range of the saint's influence, the poet can still demonstrate to us how thinking in the heart leads to God.

XVI

On being too Cheerful

WHILE FREEDOM FROM GLOOM is the natural consequence of the Christian's faith, he has still to take account of how cheerful he is going to be. Degrees in cheerfulness are not regulated strictly by logic. The man of greatest faith has not necessarily the loudest laugh. Many miss this point. They read in a book, or are told (perhaps too indiscriminately) in a lecture that Christianity is a cheerful religion, and under immediate influence of this they put on a display of hilarity as if their intention was to convince themselves and others how completely Christian they are.

Regrettable things happen as a result. Over-cheerful people, their broad countenances lit by unreflecting glee, descend upon others, who are not at all tuned to their pitch, to give them the benefits of their brotherhood. Their simple thought seems to be that, if they beam broadly on people the world is thereby made more Christian. The sensitive shudder at their approach.

The over-cheerful are no respecters of temperament or season. They are liable to turn on their heartiness no less in the aciduous morning than in that hour of greatest toleration, before sundown, when all men are hastening to forgive their enemies. They have no eye for preoccupation or indigestion in others. They are a menace to their liverish brother whose native disposition it is to acknowledge with no more than a sympathetic nod of the head the fact that Christ is risen. They seem to be showing how they think they would look if they were being thrown to the lions.

While people live at this excessive degree of cheerfulness ordinary communication with them is unsatisfactory, or even impossible. They are all taken up with setting a standard of tolerance which is quite impracticable. While the fit is on them any unpardonable folly or maddening anomaly is smiled on, and they will think you a renegade to the counsels of perfection if you interrupt their mirth to remark that the mutton is not as good as it was. Elated, it would seem, at not having here a lasting city, the super-cheerful for the moment lose touch with the fact that the city may last yet a little longer.

But the inevitable happens. They cannot keep it up. The impossible pitch of cheerfulness in the face of everything is not maintained. The city lasts longer than their mood.

As a result we have this doubling of personality which so seriously disfigures the way of some whose lives are specially dedicated to religion. Under the influence of an external stimulus (reading or preaching) they go impossibly cheerful, and not being able to keep it up they revert, with characteristic thoroughness, to the opposite state. The advantages of keeping an even keel, even in the expression of cheerfulness, have not been brought home to them; nor the old principle that in all expression we must be true to the inner self, and that it is a big mistake to seem more cheerful than we feel.

From want of true reflection we may fall under the delusion that by getting into our countenances more beaming benevolence than we really feel we will make Christianity more popular and help in the spread of the gospel. It is better policy to recall that by a level performance we avoid distressing people with a weakly-founded mirth, and save the irritable man from himself who will otherwise form an even lower opinion of us than we deserve. The wide range of expression from extreme cheerfulness to extreme gloom which some faces accomplish—apparently in the interests of Christianity—strikes one as a range which the mind itself could not accomplish.

So come about those sudden and violent readjustments of the countenance without which so many people think they cannot do their job. They do not trust their own instinct in expression of themselves. In making a style they make a face. The cheerful face and the other one have their hours on and their hours off—and sometimes the whole show is given away by their inadvertently letting us see the changing of the guard.

Christianity does not expect of a man that he shall counterfeit glee when he has lost his pocket-wallet or been trodden on in a crowd. The brave smile is an honourable performance and a fine tradition, but it can be overdone. The imitation of it looks bad. It is better to have respect for our own limitations. Singing on a broken heart is a romantic achievement designed for the stage. The introduction of it into everyday life is ill-advised. Either the singing will not be good or the heart not quite broken.

Heroic cheerfulness, while it crowns the names of some great sufferers, is still mostly legendary. It is exceptional, like the grand style. Literature has loved the pathos of it and has given us more of it than is seen in life. The pathetic figure of the professional jester striving to joke with an eye on the whip has been over-advertised and unwittingly taken as a standard. In the emergencies of grief a bearing less spectacular than mirth will be enough for glory. The king's fool, in the play, was well employed in labouring to out-jest the heart-struck injuries of his master, but he had more wisdom and sensibility than to do the same with his own.

XVII

On being a Safe Man

PRUDENCE, TOO, can run to excess, and the term, Safe Man, is a term of reproach. The safe man is of the race of men who invented the proverbs. He knows he has a good thing in the proverbs, and that the more than half-truth which they contain will not let him down. He looks before he leaps and knows the advantages of being sure over being sorry. He is principally distinguished by the fact that he is not the first by whom the new is tried, while he holds himself in exceptional readiness to profit by the enterprise of others.

Many an honest seeker after holiness who bows his head in formal meditations, searching and researching for perfection, may quite forget to suspect himself of this unattractive characteristic. Many who could not be called out-and-out safe men, who are not resented as such by their acquaintances, have yet too much of the safe man in them. The excessively prudent are not always seen to be such by those who are themselves more generous and trusting, so that, in effect, the excessively prudent prosper by imposing on the generous and the trusting. The good qualities of the safe ones, such as their agreeableness and lack of aggressiveness, dim the edges of their otherwise unfavourable outline. They are discovered in their true shape by reflection rather than by observation. Thus—to take an instance—it will not be until some time has elapsed that two people, who have been impulsive and said more than they should have said on some matter, will recall that there was a third present, equal to them in circumstance, who certainly said less than he ought to have said.

It is only to be expected that the sudden in speech should form a poor opinion of those whose prudence is extreme. For the sudden suffer the double disadvantage that they can neither stop themselves nor start the others. Without taking sides with the reckless, we can measure the exasperation which is caused in them by those in whom self-suppression works automatically like a safety catch. These are the cute. They begin nothing, they change nothing. They table no motions, they are not even seconders. They wait for the carrying unanimously.

Nor is this very thing for which they are instinctively disliked absent from their spiritual life. Here they show like children of light who have copied too much from the children of this world. Their industry is exemplary. But they are unedifying and somewhat distressing by their pre-occupation with the means rather than the end. Their anxiety is not so much with becoming something, as with being possessed of such credentials as will give St. Peter at the gate no option. Their anxiety is to be possessed of a claim, to have a bill drawn on Heaven itself, to have the promise in writing, to have a securer hold than is had by Faith and Hope.

If we could imagine a scheme of things in which The Almighty had provided us with several ways of insuring ourselves against the disadvantages of our free-will, several ways of our being able to guarantee ourselves Heaven, and if it were also explicitly laid down that any *one* of these would be sufficient to secure the end, still the safe ones, these men and women with the habit of insurance, would be found making a collection of all the guarantees.

Thrift of this kind, in which there is left none of the adventurousness of trust, has never been very popular upon earth and one is disposed to wonder how it is regarded in Heaven. The Kingdom of Heaven is indeed borne away by those who persist, but more by the use of violence than calculation.

Further, in the case against Safe Men, it is to be noted, that commonly we have owed more to those who took a chance and seemed to fail than to those who always played safe and seemed to succeed. On the ruins of the failure of yesterday the success of to-day is often built. The paradox of the man who is ahead of his time has a still finer point— the Safe Men save their age from him but he saves the succeeding age from the Safe Men.

Progress dates from the man who takes a chance. His risk implies renunciation and the hope of charity. Mere gambling apart, there is the unmistakable touch of greatness about the man who casts his bread upon the waters. Instinctively we call him unworldly—though the extent to which this is a compliment depends, naturally, on the extent of our belief in another world. The home of lost causes is a home for the spirit. It is nearly a truism to say that though movements and reforms are begun with the highest aims and the noblest intentions, they will get nowhere without martyrs—that martyrs are indeed the only guarantee of their worth. And martyrs do not come from the ranks of the Safe Men.

On a more everyday stage—below the level of that on which the martyrs and the big Safe Men move—the same contention of values goes on on a reduced scale. The little Safe Man—over-shrewd but inoffensive—is a spectator in a front seat. At his worst he is giving all his attention to the rising sun, or making arrangements for being first off the sinking ship. At his best he is keeping his counsel too strictly to himself and trading upon the saying that it is not the man who knows the most who has the most to say. Thus the little Safe Man sometimes gets a name for being deeper than he is dug.

Silence is golden, he tells himself, and holds back his opinion, even on a trifle, for no other reason than from a constitutional miserliness. Practised and comfortable in silence, to a degree far beyond what is comfortable for the normal man, the Safe Man puts to use his accomplishment. Quite at his ease, he can be silent while another, to find an equal degree of comfort, is driven to say more than he had intended to say. Even with those who suffer no embarrassment from his cautious silence the safe one will win, if winning consists in taking more than is given.

While appearing not to take advantage of others, or in any way to curtail the rights of others, the Safe Man does so in effect. He has an unfair advantage in so far as he does not run the risk of losses that arise from playing the game in the accepted way. He is all the time storing up and giving an unfair permanence to remarks in passing, and to those half-considered things which normal people in a spirit of companionship put into circulation for the moment and intend for the moment only. The silence of the safe one, while the conversation goes on, gives him more time for reflecting on it and for calculating how, by questions less innocent and more far-reaching than they seem, he may attain to a more complete revelation than would have been vouchsafed to him if he played the game on equal terms with the rest. And all the time he may consider that he is playing fair. What to others is seen as an unfair advantage taken by him, may seem to him no more than the impact of the indiscretion of the rest upon his wisdom.

Because of his silence and study of caution the Safe Man is sometimes confused with St. James's perfect man who offends not by the tongue. But close observation may show that this Safe Man who keeps a guard upon his tongue is not as righteous as he looks. He has perfected a technique of a very doubtful kind. What is the nature of his offence who, while careful to the point of scrupulosity to speak no uncharity himself, yet lives in hope that someone else will give him the pleasure of it while relieving him of the responsibility? He may go farther than that. He may keep within the law with every syllable himself, but contrive to plot the course of the conversation so that others will not. His sensitive ear suggests to him that a string which has been but lightly touched may be made to yield a lively tune, and when the time is apt he puts the speaker back upon it again.

Further, his silence and his caution make him appear to be the ideal recipient for such things as are only to be whispered. With a view to strengthening this impression and tempting others to say what they should not, the Safe Man will undertake to look a few degrees more discreet than he actually is.

Some of the very best shots of the cynic are fired at the Safe Man, but the latter does not change his style. He finds his style pays too well. What is jest for the cynic is policy for the Safe Man. For him loyalty has its limits defined. A retreat, where a stand should be made, is no more than an inconvenience. Desertion of companions is not regarded by him as a dereliction on his own part but as a failure of strategy on theirs. No word was pledged—the Safe Man is justified on paper.

He began his career of excessive circumspection in his schooldays. Unnoticed against the speed and thoughtlessness of normal boyish action he studied caution and began early to over-estimate the advantages it gave him over his fellows. He was very soon convinced of the disadvantages of principle for the sake of principle, and decided, that whatever about others *he* was not made that way. This seemed to be a constitutional way out. Independent, disinterested action, or courageous speaking from conviction when there was nothing to gain but perhaps something to lose, were always to him works of supererogation, fireworks of the spirit, conspicuous gallantry to which no man was bound.

"Certainly," wrote Bacon, "the ablest men that ever were have had all an openness and frankness of dealing, and a name of frankness and veracity . . ." But Bacon, who made no pretence of being an idealist, seeing here an opening for commercialising a virtue, adds: "When they thought the case required dissimulation, if they had then used it, it came to pass that the former opinion spread abroad, of their good faith and clearness of dealing, made them almost invincible." This is, ethically, a very low finish. To find the mean between the way of the Safe Man and the way of his opposite number, who with a distressing kind of superabundance of 'character' makes a point of fighting with his bread and butter, we must go higher than Bacon. There have been many good statements of that mean both in and out of fiction. This is as expressive as any; "Rightly to be great is not to stir without great argument, but greatly to find quarrel in a straw when honour's at the stake."

XVIII

On Calling a Bore a Bore

OUR NEIGHBOUR BEING SO MUCH the burden of conversation, the eternal problem is to be interesting without being uncharitable. The generality of people in their conversation are not aiming at being 'bright' exactly, but they have a hope of being in some way entertaining—and their 'neighbour,' they know, is the only subject they can be entertaining upon. Without the neighbour, conversation will languish and life will not be worth living. It might be contended that of none of their obligations do people remain more aware than this of not speaking uncharitably of their neighbour. Many converse to the end of their days in a state of semi-frustration, half-way between good faith and bad. Getting near the bone of the absent neighbour, they will preface with "One doesn't like being uncharitable," or, having actually touched the neighbour's bone, they will say "Of course we mustn't be uncharitable," as if this postscript had some virtue in it.

This sensitiveness to the obligation of speaking charitably commonly gets a queer result. Thus, many people begin by interpreting their obligation with an excessive strictness, and then, finding the strain too much for them, they completely break through the law as properly interpreted. They react very badly to the strain of trying to see more in their neighbour than is there—which they wrongly imagine to be their obligation. Those who labour under this misconception will most likely also imagine that humility means estimating themselves as worse than they are. The double strain of trying to see less in themselves and more in their neighbour than is there soon proves to be too much for them.

If Private Brown is of opinion that the sergeant-major is a very holy man, Private Murphy is entitled to say that he has not noticed it—if he has not. If, on the other hand, Private Murphy is convinced that the sergeant-major is a very holy man, he is well within the bounds of charity if he still gives it as his opinion that the sergeant-major makes only a very poor shot at sergeant-majoring. The sergeant-major will not have to answer at the Judgment Day for not being able to shout as loud in the barrack-square as a sergeant-major whom Private Murphy knew in Mhow. It is only the imperfections that will be on the agenda on Judgment Day that entertainment must stop short of.

This is labouring the obvious, but the prevalence of the misconception nearly justifies it. Persons with a ridiculously false conscience in the matter can be heard making some pointless remark about being uncharitable at the mere mention of the name of someone who is not present. This kind of thing makes some of the company jumpy, and makes others determined to be uncharitable as a kind of protest against the abnormality.

Housekeeping and the rearing of children are, for instance, either arts or sciences, and if certain mothers in discussion use the case of an absent neighbour to indicate a degree of attainment in these arts or sciences well below the highest, they are not necessarily being uncharitable. But a foolish member of the party with a false conscience may come to thinking that the moral mark has been crossed; and, deciding that she may as well be hung for a sheep as a lamb, she will make the first really uncharitable remark.

Another instance of false conscience in this matter is found in the case of the person who has developed a quite excessive fear of being what he calls *critical*. He will have gathered from some authority, who has not in fact given the business sufficient thought, that every urge to criticise is to be resisted; that it is to be regarded as evidence of a lack of the 'proper spirit,' a lack of good will. A preacher or writer, in a moment of thoughtlessness or foolish enthusiasm, will have gone clean against the judgments of common sense and suggested that the person in a community who criticises the running of it is no more than a grumbler and a grouser. As a result of this wrong view some who have commented adversely, but quite justifiably, on the cooking or the need for paint will nonsensically accuse themselves of speaking uncharitably. A real danger is that if the duty of expressing justifiable criticism is neglected by members of a community, out of a mistaken idea that all such is grumbling, then the standard of efficiency which all ought to strive for may be lowered. Superiors and all those who are in a high station—it follows logically—have good reason to keep watch on themselves lest they begin to call that uncharity which is only fair comment.

The subject of Bores cannot be separated from any discussion on uncharitable speaking. Bores have been classified according to the different 'lines' they take and according to the different ways in which the victim experiences discomfort from them. The crashing Bore, the drilling Bore, the corrosive Bore and the rest of them are very real phenomena. To talk of a Bore, and at the same time to avoid all mention of that particular quality by which he is fixed in our minds, represents a degree of detachment to which the mass of people have not the slightest claim.

Bores are born not made. That a man has exceptional powers of boring is a fact which we do not hold him responsible for more than we do for his having weak sight or a defective memory. Or, to be more precise, the peculiarity in his make-up by which he becomes a Bore is not related any more closely to his moral being than is some distressing mannerism which he may possess, such as an unfortunate way of laughing.

It will not be uncharitable then to include amongst the qualities of Mr. So and So the fact that he is a Bore, belonging to this or that category. In certain cases there may even be an obligation in charity to call attention to the fact, forewarning those whom we know to be fitted with the poorest possible resistance to Bores of Mr. So and So's particular type. Account must be taken that in this noisy and nervy age many people are very ill-fitted for being nice to Bores. Timely warnings will conduce to the general harmony of life.

It will be only ordinary wisdom on the part of the recipient of the warning to suspend judgment on the unknown Bore, especially if he who gives the warning happens to be a Bore himself.

Charity is sensible as well as courteous. If Charity does not go out of its way to call a spade a spade, neither does it go out of its way to pretend that a spade is something other than a spade. It is not the way of Charity to blindfold herself in conversation and yet seek to squint beneath the folds. Charity does not harden the heart and seek to mend matters by putting a finger to her lips.

So often our way is crabbed and out of proportion— a sensitiveness to faults (often not faults at all) of our tongue going along with a remarkable insensitiveness to the uncharitable deed. There is a danger that we derive an excessive sense of justification from guarding the tongue. We may not see the wood for the trees. For wherever charity begins, we know it ends only where one man gives his life for another. The bigger issues will control the less. An awareness of the larger manifestations and commands of charity will best set the pace for our tongues. Charity is bigness of mind swallowing up littleness, not scrupling to call a man a bore and being ready, at the same time, to die for him.

XIX

On Religion and Good Manners

MOST OF US PROBABLY think our manners good enough, if indeed we ever reflect on them at all. A few points of exactness, perhaps, might be supplied from the book. More poise too, would be welcome. But poise we reckon an innate gift; so there is not much to be done but wish we had been born with more of it. And beyond that we do not go.

People who make formal meditations towards the attainment of spiritual perfection do not have Good Manners, as a subject, in their meditation book. It would be thought too trifling in the table of contents beside the usual array of things. For despite so many household words about the importance of good manners they are not really accepted as being in a grade above superficialities. The poet's saying that "The grace of God is in courtesy" is an attractive saying, and the religious man will recognise it as such. But the religious man will hardly bring it into his meditation on grace. And yet there is authority for his doing so. For a saint, and a very considerable saint, too, has said that "Holiness is politeness sanctified."

We all know pretty well how far politeness can be reduced to a mere mechanism. When men joke about having an automatic device for hat-raising we know they have slipped for the moment from the high standard of the saint. But without any jokes being made, and in a much wider field of activity than that of hat-raising, an unfailing mechanism may unfortunately come to be substituted for an unfailing thoughtfulness. A common cause of our failure to turn ourselves into saints by the exercise of politeness is our tendency to limit our expressions of politeness to those who are our equals or our betters.

A first-class meditation might be made on the feelings of servants. To help to fix the mind on the subject some striking scene involving disregard of a servant's feelings might be taken. This need not be fabulous. Ordinary observation of life will supply it.

"Man's inhumanity to man" does not refer to wars only. If the waiter happens to be a normally sensitive man, you may see the saying fulfilled any moment in a hotel lounge. A customer before giving his order may indulge in a little smartness, sharpening his wit upon the waiter for the benefit of the party. The unfairness to the waiter is evident to the party. But this man is a strong character and the party cannot do much about it. They counterfeit uneasy mirth because they find it more easy to offend the waiter than to appear not to appreciate their friend.

The unwelcome humour (and with it the implication that, as one pays the bill one is entitled to the liberty) is of the kind for which a man would be struck by an equal. But patience means too much to the waiter. You will notice him take the wound behind a hastily improvised mask of indifference, or—which is a sadder sight—see him feign appreciation of the customer's wit as he goes about the order. His feelings are wiped out for a living. We should remind ourselves how grossly inadequate is the comment so frequently heard about a happening like this, namely the comment that 'these men have their feelings too.' This virtuous comment, when we look into it, is itself an amazing sort of revelation. It is virtue to the mind that speaks it. And yet the height of this virtue is no more than a grudging admission that human feeling also exists below the two hundred pound a year mark.

Thoughtlessness is an insufficient defence at any time. Obviously it will not do at all for those who are aiming at perfection. Yet it is something to reflect upon that we are forced to fall back on it as an excuse for the behaviour of many whose profession is holiness. We are thinking of those times when they show an imperfect awareness of others, when nothing about them would suggest to us that their holiness is politeness sanctified.

When we have in mind not any one of the scenes from the life of Christ, but instead that somewhat familiar picture of him which through many years has formed itself within us; when our imagination sets before us its image of him as he came and went amongst those who were well acquainted with him and those whom he was meeting for the first time, amongst those who were gracious and those who were not; when we are seeing him with a kind of second sight, seeing him not as the doer of several things in several scenes but as one whose way gives such satisfying consistency to all the scenes; when, in a word, we are under the immediate influence of the 'manner' of Christ, what an automatic correction it is for manners that we had come to think were good enough because we felt that they were better than much that we saw around us.

Mention of the considerateness of Christ may bring to mind the text about the bruised reed and the smoking flax. It is a text which usually appears in such a context as this— but we might reflect how here, as in other cases, the poetic text is a distraction to us. Soothed by the spell of the poetry we rather miss the point. For it is not unusual with us to escape logical consequence by the use of poetry. So, in citing this particular text, we may echo the words with a sort of routine tenderness and yet scarcely look beyond the metaphor. We may experience the soothing quality of the words but have no fresh realization of the particular ways in which the considerateness of Christ showed itself in relation, not to reeds and flax, but to the faces and feelings of men.

Interest is the quality in good manners which many fail at having who have all the rest. Fineness of feeling is based on an interest in things. To be of value it must, naturally, be unaffected interest. To be consistently present it must be supported by such a complete lack of egoism as is rarely to be found. The highest compliment to a thing is to be interested in it. It was the way of Christ to pay to all creation a continuous compliment. The inconsiderate person is remarkable for failing at a compliment or paying a forced one. His egotism sharply limits his interests. The spectacle of small things has no power to force him into thoughtfulness. He could be in the temple for ever and not see the widow's mite. His way is brusque or unnoticing, never tentative enough. He is without the tact which is a consciousness of one's surroundings and a true report on them. The inconsiderate man has not a hope of that perfectly managed adjustment to the scene which depends on having the right degree of interest in it and which is the distinctive quality in the man who is noted for his manners.

Strange though it sounds, there is a type of bad manners specifically associated with persons who are making a special effort to dedicate themselves to religion. The fault is one of aggressiveness, traceable to a sort of selfishness or acquisitiveness in acquiring spiritual goods. If it were possible to suppose these goods limited in quantity, then the people here spoken of would have to be proceeded against for seeking more than their just share. As it is, they must be censured for their spiritual style. In their good works they have about them a competitive air. They look like people who have some valuable inside information but are determined to keep it to themselves. They acquire the bearing of successful collectors. By their very purposefulness they can make an expression of hope and trust from gentler folk sound like mere improvidence.

Such a one is he whose bee-line for his soul's salvation is such as to leave upon our minds the impression that the salvation of others is but a very poor second with him indeed. He is the spiritual counterpart of the man who sees nobody else's plight until he has shouldered his way into the bus, and is then prepared to do anything to get the rest in, except get out himself.

May it be hinted—with all the delicacy that such a matter requires—that there shows in some good people a hint of aggressiveness which seems traceable, however inappropriately, to a consciousness that they are in the state of grace? 'Consciousness' is hardly the word, for they would know better than to feel so sure of themselves. But there is some kind of overflow of aggressiveness into their actions and it seems to be coming from springs of self-righteousness.

Doors, for instance, are much more likely to be banged by the righteous than by those who do not feel so sure of themselves. I take this seeming trifle, because doors, when you consider them well, are an excellent test of thoughtfulness. We are constantly encountering them and always at those times when our consideration for others tends to be at its lowest. The Ego is in its most unmodified form when we are at the door. It has either drawn itself off completely from one company or has not fallen under the influence of another.

There is much symbolism about the door and the threshold. On many, however, the symbolism appears to be lost— and some, in their dealings with the door, add significations of their own. A thorough-going banger of doors not only signals his departure from a room by the noise he makes but also makes it clear that he thinks there is not much point in being there after he has left. Notable door-bangers have certain variations of their style. They will not only bang doors on their way in but leave them open on their way out, giving double proof of their purely personal interest in apartments. As a further variation they will use the open door as a place for reading letters or for saying all the things that had not occurred to them when they were in the room proper. It is useless to put aside charity, and hope they will catch a chill from the draught. Practice has acclimatised them. It is we who get the chill.

The first places are often sought as keenly in the church as at the table. This is not necessarily from want of humility (for there is a sort of understanding between the righteous themselves that, within the sacred edifice, humility shall not be reckoned according to the place selected.) The pressure on the best seats is due entirely to considerations of their practical value, to considerations of the greater spiritual profit to be had from them—if the preacher has a poor delivery, for instance. The thought that there are not sufficient best seats for everyone is in most ways an unpractical and useless thought—the only ones who can derive any profit from it will be those who happen to have the best seats.

A man can look quite selfish in a corner seat, even when he has an undisputed claim to it, even when he is praying. Or he can look altogether unselfish there, if he be of the right spirit. Instead of looking as if he had circumvented or beaten everyone else to it, and was prepared to defend it against all comers, he may look as if his being there was the result of a conspiracy on the part of the others to put him there. The spirit is everything. The humble and considerate will in turn take their place at the top and at the bottom without either affectation or embarrassment. And while they know that the violent bear away the kingdom of heaven, their own violence will never become aggressiveness, or give to their good works that questionable sort of thoroughness which owes so much to an imperfect awareness of the fate of others.

XX

On being Merciful

WE ARE ALL GOOD at not grinding the faces of the poor. Secure, too, in not having the responsibility of administering justice we take for preference the lenient view. In fact it is hard to think of any commandment in respect of which we feel more righteous than we do about the commandment to be merciful.

But not less noticeable than our righteousness is our delusion that mercy belongs only to rather special sorts of occasions or to very important persons. We look in the headlines to see if Mercy has been honoured, and forget to consider whether the stamp of it is upon the small change of our own lives. Our general intent is to be merciful. Vaguely we are thinking of how, in some exceptional circumstances, we would do the big thing, how we would decide, for instance, not to take the law of someone despite severe injury and provocation. In such an exceptional case the likelihood is that the thing would go to our heads and we would not be able to resist the attractiveness of making a display of magnanimity in public.

Well-known sayings about being merciful as well as strong, and about mercy becoming the throned monarch better than his crown, help to strengthen the delusion that mercy has only to do with very big men. The poor, the weak and the common people lose sight of an obligation to be merciful. Throughout the petty performances which are the most of their history there is not much thought of the gentle rain falling upon the place beneath.

The delusion does not stop at the plain man. It will be

found with the dedicated. Men and women whose aim is to copy into their lives the Christian counsels of perfection steel themselves so that they shall, when their hour comes, have mercy and not sacrifice. They, too, are thinking of some exceptional time and circumstance. They have in mind some dramatic moment when they will remember Christ's lesson and go one better than the Good Samaritan. But their lives pass, and they never find themselves riding down from Jerusalem to Jericho.

They meet no case so desperate as that of the man who fell amongst robbers, and so their reservoirs of mercy do not get turned on. Which means that they are kept turned off. Life is lived without the exercise of mercy. Favourable occasions for the exercise of the virtue are not seen to be such, so little have they to do with pouring in oil and binding up wounds. Content to think that, if the great chance should come their way they would wear mercy like a jewel, hardly a day passes that they do not add to the world's pain.

Consider one of life's very familiar miseries. Consider how many are the boys and girls—the able as well as the dull—who carry through life an embittered memory of their schooldays, because someone kept mercy turned off. The memory lives with particular bitterness when the lack of mercy is associated with a man or woman whose religious calling implied the unfailing manifestation of it. Back to the mind, through all the years after, as often as the name of some teacher or superior is mentioned, comes the memory of some persecution of the schooldays. It may be the memory of one single act of cruelty—it may be only one word spoken, but it hurts for ever.

Unnecessary hurt, treatment with even but a tinge of cruelty in it, leaves a curious mark upon the mind of the adolescent. It makes more difficult the making of friends and even the approach to God.

Some with a great fame for the rectitude of their lives go very lightly and unthinkingly over this very matter. Just here conscience weakens in them; their very 'effectiveness' is based to some extent on their unawareness of, or their indifference to, the fact that mercy is always in season. These 'strong' and 'effective' characters nearly succeed in setting up a new standard of conduct. Their renown for goodness and zeal, and especially their fame for 'not sparing themselves,' seem almost to entitle them to pursue inhuman ways. A sort of ruthlessness begins to look like a virtue through its association with their obvious excellences. They do 'great work'; and they can make a paragraph like this sound very trifling.

It does seem but a trifle when the very efficient master (whom everyone praises—and with so much good reason) cuts a boy to the quick or sours him by an unfairness. The spotlight is on the master, the boy's case is unnoticed. The trifle may be any of a hundred things. A familiar one is the master's first making the mistake of inviting something like competition from the pupil, and then, when things are not going to his liking, treating the successful attitude of the pupil as if it had something of insubordination in it. When he grows to be a man, it is true that the boy will be the better able to see that the matter was only a trifle. But he will also have an intensified rather than a reduced sensation of the unfairness that was associated with it.

Even those excellent people who are credited with 'doing great work for God' should not fail to reflect that they may be fulfilling the law and the prophets with great personal inconvenience to others, no less than to themselves. The seeker after perfection according to the book—the quite honest and singleminded seeker of it—may be having an influence on the lives of others that is nothing short of terrifying.

Mercy does not seem to be as practical as many of the other subjects in the book of formal meditations, not so applicable to daily life. And so it happens that there is not much to prevent a policy of thoroughness from becoming a policy of ruthlessness. Progress is thought of as solely by way of the bee-line. So important is it to get from Jerusalem to Jericho, so much is this alone viewed as important, that there is no allowance for any stops on the way.

Those who have reason to suspect themselves of being either zealous or efficient must in a very special way examine their talent for being merciful. And this is most important in the early morning when the efficient or zealous one is setting out to maintain his reputation for another day. The possible victims are now lined up, and the pull of human nature is towards sacrifice. Whether it is to be mercy or sacrifice will soon be revealed in the use and emphasis of the pronoun "I." Efficiency, as this world knows, goes with both mercy and sacrifice—but more usually with the latter. With the very best intentions may go plain cruelty.

If you are strong be merciful. We who are of frail constitution, and neither Kings nor Judges, are apt to miss the point. For mercy is a quality of the mind, anyone's mind. Let a man be powerless and insignificant, there is still some small world in which he can hurt like a tyrant. A man may never raise his hand, or even his voice, and still be a tyrant in his speech. He may be punctilious in avoiding calumny and yet be remarkably unmerciful in his conversation, one who lessens in others their relish for humanity. The charge against him is not that he fails to suffer fools gladly or that he is too sudden or devastating in his attacks upon humbug.

It is rather that by his opinions he lowers the heart without cause. He has grown to like the bad taste in his own mouth. He likes to help in the spread of disillusionment for its own sake. He is not as honourable as the pessimist; for as gloom is the vocation of the pessimist, it is with this man only a profession. This man makes the genial mind shudder; when he speaks, the sum of the world's goodness contracts. His opposite is not the optimist or the cheerful man. His opposite is the merciful man, who in his spirit of tolerance reflects God's own appreciation for the things He has made.

Being merciful is of its nature a chivalrous and romantic performance. It involves delay, it is a 'loss of time.' This unpractical quality of mercy makes it less acceptable in a state of civilisation which can be described—without taking sides—as highly geared. Though there may not be more wise men about than formerly, it is certainly much easier to look a fool. The changes that have come to pass since the days of Saint Francis of Assisi make the taking off of one's coat in the street and giving it to a beggar more difficult to explain than it was in his time. It is now felt to be necessary to 'explain it away.' And certainly we are far too ready with the word 'eccentricity' to explain it.

It is now so long a time since Francis lived that his graciousness has about it the added charm of antiquity, and the reports of his deeds are assimilated by the mind with a ready welcome as if they were coming to it from the realms of poetry and romance. But this very charm is a danger, because it hides the plain realism of the saint's acts, even from those who fancy themselves as realists. There is no need to look for a poetic streak in Francis in order to explain him. The explanation of him is that he was consistently merciful. That a habit of mercy could so far distinguish a man amongst his fellows is a pointer in more ways than one. The consistently merciful man does not happen often. Probably it was due to his merciful mind that Francis earned his grand and peculiar fame that he reminded men of Christ.

XXI

On being Grateful

ABOUT THE FIRST LESSON which parents teach their children is the importance of saying 'thanks.' With this social grace secured, the sign of civilization is set. The expression of gratitude, from such constant use, has become as mechanical as anything else in our speech. 'Thank-you' and 'Thanks' run off our tongue without any new effort of the mind. Nor do those more complicated expressions such as 'This is most sweet of you' necessarily mean more.

This is not said carpingly. Indeed it might be argued that if the flow of life is not to be seriously interrupted some ready mechanism for expressing thanks is necessary. Engrossed, for instance, in talking to or listening to a friend in a bus, we cannot very well use more than our mechanical 'thank-you' when the conductor gives us our ticket. Still less can anyone expect the conductor to make special and personal acts of gratitude to his passengers thousands of times per day.

If people in the mass were suddenly to be overcome by a lively sense of gratitude about lots of things that are now disposed of by ordinary automatic expression, there would be a general slowing down of pace, a universal speechlessness. People would then not be able to hurry away with gifts and favours so expeditiously as convention now allows; their feelings would be more unspeakable and they would take longer to recover from them. Perfection of the virtue would cause much dislocation. Heaven has to provide for such problems. On earth there is no fear of dislocation. By the conventional formula thanks is always implied. And even if the mind is, ordinarily, inattentive to what it is expressing, still it does from time to time reflect upon the fact that gratitude is a good thing, and from the reflection subsequent mechanical expressions derive virtue.

But blessed are they in whom the virtue shows stronger than this—they who have won renown by their gratitude. They have it both ways. They have it a hundred ways. Their concept of what goodness is is enlarged until it is nearly too much for the mind to hold. They discover spiritual spaces and altitudes by the rest undreamt of. They see into the life of things without undergoing the fatigue of being poets. They have the enoblement of humility without undergoing humiliation.

Philosophers know that being is better than non-being. If a philosopher has a special turn for gratitude he can go straight into an ecstasy over the fact that he has been born.

So may a sense of gratitude work quite naturally and logically in an unbeliever, until it leads him the whole way from unbelief to God and to his soul's salvation. His eye begins to be taken by the spectacle of goodness in so many places, high up and low down. He feels gratitude for what he owns and what he shares with others, counting up all things, rejoicing even in abstractions like line and colour. He is thrilled by the companionship of his friends. He finds that he is loved and becomes speechless. Then he looks for someone to thank for it all. For these things are plainly to him *gifts*. He is aware of them as things passing between someone and himself. He does not for a moment be so remiss as to take them for granted. His whole life is motivated by the thought that he has nothing that he has not received. He is as logical as he is happy. He looks around for someone to thank, and discovers God.

Poor-spirited familiarity dims our sight. Gratitude gives back the vision. The poet could have wished himself a pagan of the old world that the voice of nature might sound better in his ear. He might with more point have wished for the gratitude of the Christian saint upon whose consciousness all things swarm as the gifts of God, making him the legatee of all creation, and teaching him, as Francis was taught, the language of the birds.

It is the measure of our imperfect gratitude that though all this is logical it sounds fantastical. He who praises the greenness of the grass and gives thanks for it is thought to be going too far, and he may not do it at all unless with the excuse that he is writing poetry.

But even things that are much more obviously *gifts* than the greenness of the grass we, in our dull unappreciative way, take for granted. What gratitude they awaken in us is not worth talking about. Indeed, if we do not at intervals shake ourselves into a better state of realization and begin again from scratch, we not only lose our sense of gratitude but even become incapable of the common joy of receiving. What of the impression made upon us by what seem to be those routine gifts at Christmas time? We forget that someone began thinking of something 'nice' for us as early as the middle of October, looked in the shop-windows constantly for two whole months, thought of a hundred things and rejected them, played with the thought of every conceivable thing for us, and finally with a megrim in the head on Christmas Eve went and bought us gloves again. And we see in them only another pair of gloves.

Giving, as the wise know, is its own reward. Though the mind of the giver may not be full of a higher motive, satisfactory feelings are still promoted in him by the very act of giving. Ingratitude in the receiver does of course cast its shadow on the performance. And not always are the most generous givers the most thanked. Perhaps the paradox could be maintained that they are the least.

Custom stales. The person who gives most readily is in time considered by those who benefit from him to be just that sort of person. His gifts, because they are frequent, are taken for granted. Much is discounted from the generosity of the rich because they are rich. They never satisfy the ungrateful, who argue (conveniently) that if they were themselves rich they would give so much more. Which is not proved.

So comes about one of the unadvertised sadnesses of the rich, and of God. Go through the gospel seeking what, to your thinking, was for Christ the most disappointing moment in His life. Quick to recur to the mind will be those times of sadness about momentous things as when He wept over Jerusalem, or of sadness with momentous sequel as when the disciples said it was a hard saying and many of them walked with Him no more. But there were other times less conspicuous than these, less observed, hardly heeded even by those around him, though full of significance for them if they should afterwards reflect on them, and full of poignancy to this day for all who read the story of them closely. Such a time was that when ten lepers were healed and only one (the outsider of the group) returned to give thanks.

The one returning out of ten adds peculiar pathos. He is the tattered shred that gratitude so often is, there being so often no more than will serve to call attention to ingratitude. The disappointment of Christ is the disappointment of all with the means to give who go on giving generously, their gifts taken for granted, whose very generosity involves them in seeing something more of the frailty and meanness of humanity than they would otherwise see.

The healed lepers did not *think*, we say—anticipating a

defence for our own ingratitudes. Custom, we add, had sealed their eyes to the vision of goodness diffusing itself. Custom has indeed much to answer for. But amongst its worst offences is that it has bred the saying 'small thanks to him,' and even extended the saying to God.

XXII

On not wearing a Hair-Shirt

WHEN A MAN IS SEEN twisting his neck about and experiencing discomfort with his collar and tie, the last thing anyone suspects is that he is having trouble with his hair-shirt. I make this seemingly-frivolous statement because it is a help to realising by what unpassable chasms the general run of people believe their lives to be separated from the life that is called Ascetical. The mass of ordinary, good-living people see themselves as out of all relation to the ascetical life and see those who follow it as members of another race. Many of these same ordinary people, may, in fact, be having a very trying life, a life full of privations, with no relaxation in it worth talking about, and no hope to the end of their days of escape from a relentless machine of somebody else's making. But they never think—and do not want to think—that this life of theirs is in any way the material equivalent of a hair-shirt.

The man trained in spirituality is tempted to tell—and very frequently does tell—these harrassed folk about the splendid opportunity they have of deriving from the daily round the spiritual benefits which the Ascetic, as such, gets from his hair-shirt. For the man trained in spirituality simply cannot take his eye off this opportunity. 'Make virtue of necessity,' he says again and again; 'offer it all up, spiritualize it.' But the good plain people want to remain plain; they shrink from this plan of spiritualizing their lives by living them from a higher motive. They have a real and constant fear of being turned into anything exceptional.

They are not afraid of suffering, they are not afraid of holiness, but they are afraid of the name of holiness.

The shrinking is not a straight case of humility. The ordinary man (as I continue to call him for want of a better name) is not deterred so much by the thought of wearing a hair-shirt as by the thought that he could not wear it and still be an ordinary man. He may be very religious but he holds back firmly from anything like 'going in for religion.' His life may be full of the self-denial that he is told about in the sermons, but he will not admit it, even to himself. It would be too like stepping out of class, he feels. Even as he listens to the preacher, he skips away from this word, 'self-denial,' treating it with respect, but treating it as a technical term, leaving it severely to holy people as a class.

In some indirect and indistinct way—to be apprehended in heaven rather than on earth—the plain man does, no doubt, succeed in spiritualizing what he continues to call the 'hard tack.' But from anything like recognisable equipment of the ascetical life he carefully keeps his distance.

Perhaps it all sounds like the paradox of the meek who are too meek to possess the land. The reticence, however, is not unfounded; it is well-intentioned. And where this reticence does tend to become extreme, the cause of it can frequently be traced—where it seldom is traced—to the unattractive spectacle presented by some who go the wrong way about becoming ascetics.

The ordinary man has not failed to notice the lack of balance which makes these unsuccessful and unattractive. He notes how they turn to the extraordinary means of asceticism before they have made the most of the ordinary means, and how they end by leading lives which could easily have been more normal without being less holy. The ordinary man never quite gets over the distressing peculiarity of their style, the painful tension, the preoccupation which is so like grimness. It is not for him, he feels, to pass any criticism on those dedicated ones who are endeavouring more than himself. But it is a point that their efforts only cause him to adhere the more to his own notions about the relation of holiness with normality. While the obvious order of things is that the Ascetic should preach to the ordinary man, it would not be wholly without profit for the Ascetic that he should sometimes hear what the ordinary man thinks about him.

It is clearly a wise precaution to suspect ourselves when we find ourselves inclined to disapprove of things recorded in the lives of the saints. At the same time if there is room for a second opinion it is better that it should be expressed. It is told, for instance, of certain holy men that they endeavoured to increase their mortifications by never changing their clothes. We can hardly be blamed if on reading this we are not able to share the enthusiasm of the writer recording it. Indeed we lose all sympathy with this particular act of mortification when we think of the effects of it upon those who lived in close contact with the holy man; and our sympathy with the biographer is grievously shortened because he could so completely disregard the feelings of those who changed their clothes regularly but had to live with one who never did.

It is related of the Curé of Ars that his fellow priests in the diocese were offended by his appearing at a conference disreputably clad. The biographer, with that uncritical enthusiasm for his subject which has done so much dis-service to hagiology, concentrates entirely on the unreason-ableness of the clergy. The Curé thought it was the more meritorious way, and the other priests evidently thought it was not. The weight of the opinion—amongst the saints as well as amongst the sinners—is here against the Curé, if we are to judge by practice.

A saint who appears in clothes plainly disreputable and unbecoming his station acts in this as in all else he does from the love of God. But others (including some saints) will feel that they are not departing from the love of God in giving it as their opinion that he ought to be better dressed. Nor is there warrant for concluding that God who so clothed the lilies of the field is specially worshipped by the wearing of disreputable clothes on a reputable occasion.

If a saint be required to refute a saint we have Francis of Sales on the side of the well-dressed. "It is a kind of contempt of those with whom we converse to come into their company in unseemly apparel," he writes. It is hardly necessary to add that he advises against "affectation, vanity, strangeness or levity" in dress, for this is only what good taste would advise. Far from advising that people striving after higher sanctity should indicate their spirit of detachment by display of poverty or eccentricity in their attire, he rather says: "For my part, I desire that devout people, whether men or women, should be the best clad in any company."

Like the several other expressions of the art of living, asceticism must be controlled by a sense of measure, a sense of proportion, by a sense of humour even. The art of concealing art is of particular importance for the ascetic. If his hair-shirt is not a good fit, he had better not wear it. The first anxiety of the successful ascetic is to see that his asceticism is not getting in the way of others.

The unsuccessful, the inartistic, ascetic is liable to the danger of thinking his asceticism the more important because it happens to be *his*. He may unduly reduce his respect for a scheme of life which is not ordered to such high ends as his own. From his long practice of very early rising he may have induced himself into thinking that there is actually a spiritual quality in the air at five or six in the morning which has been absorbed out of it by nine or ten o'clock, or even eight o'clock. The mere fact of being on his feet and in his clothes—before any supernatural motive has come into play—may seem to him to have a kind of goodness in it, which, however, he would not dream of allowing to bakers and night-watchmen.

The ascetic who fails, fails through lack of rationality. He will not have considered enough that rational asceticism is made difficult by that complexity in our nature, which, if it is allowed, will induce us to cross and baulk ourselves for a morbid sort of satisfaction that can be found in doing so. The law of the spirit versus the law of the members is a plain and recognisable conflict. The complexities within the spirit itself are more difficult. It is possible to slip into a mechanical way of countermanding our first thoughts because they presented themselves first, the presumption being that we cannot have exercised due self-control if there has not been some evidence of conflict. On this system the second part of us to enter the conflict has a big chance of being given the victory arbitrarily.

XXIII

On Saying Good-Bye

IT IS NOT MERELY the sentimental soul that, at a sad parting, cares only for its own loneliness. People with quite respectable control of their feelings may, at such a time, regard all considerations but the one as an intrusion. Those who come forward to console will do no good unless they begin with the thought that nothing can be done because a world has now about ended. Though this fact is so obvious, consolers, and even professional consolers, frequently miss it. They begin in the middle, forgetting that sorrow must be respected before there is talk of hope.

At the time of a parting which hurts there is no adequate balm—for the good reason that there is no such thing as a substitute. Nor does Christianity require of us to disregard this human truth. The unreflecting, whose consolings are marred by abruptness, seem to think that it does. They keep coming with futile words, making the eternal mistake— the mistake of telling the schoolboy returning after the Christmas holidays that he will not feel Easter coming. But there are no substitutes. Everything else said before the train leaves or the boat sails is in hopeless competition with that truth.

If he who is going away happens to be a better philosopher than those he is leaving behind, he has an added difficulty; for there is some obligation on him to try and increase their philosophy from his own, so that thought may mercifully lessen feeling.

It is not to be imagined that Christ, when going to his

death, parted from the apostles without experiencing this very difficulty. They in the sadness that came upon them at the mention of His going were farther removed than usual from the reach of philosophic considerations. Throughout the last farewell talk to them he was faced all the time with their growing depression.

Gathering to the supper that evening they had been very much their old selves, with those familiar expressions of their individualities coming and going in look and gesture —noticeable amongst these looks and gestures (certainly to Him who had so often noted it) that outward sign of their sense of possession of Him, showing most when they were gathered, as now, for a special occasion. Their unawareness of what was coming had its pathos for Him, as such awareness has for all who have in their keeping news with which they must soon sadden their friends.

When He told them He was going to leave them the life went out of them, even as it had not when He told them that one of them was about to betray Him. This parting looked so like the end of everything. They hardly asked Him *where* He was going, so little did anything matter beside the fact that He was going. Peter asked. And though the answer received could not have seemed any more satisfactory to the rest than it did to Peter, none of them pursued it. It is easy to feel the dejection of that silent company. And it is only being sympathetic with them—and not at all to crow over them—to add that the farewell then spoken, and which to us is chapter and verse, did not enter into the bowed heads who heard it with as much force as it has since entered the consciousness of many reading it.

Our odd nature is capable of feeling a grievance with those who are leaving us, even when we know that they must go. Though we may overcome this contrariness we are still slow to bring our minds in line with the farewell being said. As Christ looked from one to another of the Apostles and saw them downcast, he said, "Do not let your heart be distressed; as you have faith in God, have faith in me." But they were still distressed. No doubt at a later time the memory of these words, when they had become loaded for them with significance, could lift up their hearts. But when they were first spoken they did not lift them up, nor did they lighten for Him at all that difficulty of making access to their minds which He felt, as all feel it whose place it is to reason with grief.

When at His word they rose from the table, and by the very act of standing up felt that the end was still nearer, their depression deepened. As if meeting this additional emergency of their sadness He continues to speak while they stand ready to go. All that words can ever do to make a parting not a parting was done then, as the assurance of His closeness to them flowered into the intimacy that the vine has with its branches. The wonderful words would thrill each one of them through all the years after. But just then they thought of nothing but the parting; and, quite dejected, they followed Him from the room.

Faith can bridge the gap between a parting and a reunion to be, but the bridges faith can make will not bear the body up. The consoling of our fellow-men will be but poorly done by us if the limitations of humanity are not well remembered. The nearest we can ever go to giving the work a divine touch is not to neglect the human touch. When we rather solemnly address ourselves with 'Man, know thyself,' and survey our faults, predominant and otherwise, it is well to remember that by still other limitations and pathetic inabilities we are also made native to the earth.

The fact that hope is a virtue does not make a vice of disappointment. That we cannot get our weary bodies over the bridges which faith and hope build is neither an argument against the bridges or the bodies: they just were not made for one another. We come back again to the paradox that the recognition of our inconsolable state is the only way by which consolation can begin to be brought to us. Silence —in so far as it is a sign that others share our helplessness— may give us ease where a recited formula will sound unreal or even inhuman.

The soul of man is not always poised for flight to a better land. A cold formulatic reminder that he has not here a lasting city, while given with admirable purpose, may not improve a man's disposition. He knows he has not here a lasting city, and by the power of his faith he has firmly gripped the truth that when he comes to the lasting city it will be snagless and will overtop the reach of the senses, as Saint Paul has said. Meantime this life is a city, though neither lasting nor snagless, and a man's affection for it makes the thought of parting from it not palatable.

In this there is no need to look for insubordination or refusal of the divine will. There are kinder explanations that are sufficient. Neither need there be surprise or disappointment if the metaphors of consolation get a cool reception.

When a man sets out to 'better himself' in life it is still with some reluctance—if he be a man of heart—that he leaves that life, lower in the scale, to which he had become attached. That he *knows* he is going to better himself does not prevent him looking back even as he goes. It is only fair to him to read the looking back as a compliment to the good left behind rather than as a lack of appreciation for the better which lies ahead. To be reluctant to die to the city that is not lasting is still a compliment to God's creation.

We like to think that God looked with more sympathy than some whose sanctity chills us a little at Charles Lamb's reflections on the New Year. "In proportion," says Lamb (in a style, by the way, strangely un-secularist), "as the years both lessen and shorten, I set more account upon their periods, and would lay my ineffectual finger upon the spoke of the great wheel. I am not content to pass away 'like a weaver's shuttle.' Those metaphors solace me not . . . I am in love with this green earth—the face of town and country —the unspeakable rural solitudes, and the sweet security of streets. I would set up my tabernacle here. I am content to stand still at the age to which I am arrived, I and my friends —to be no younger, no richer, no handsomer. I do not want to be weaned by age; or drop, like mellow fruit, as they say, into the grave. Any alteration, on this earth of mine, in diet or in lodging, puzzles and discomposes me . . . A new state of being staggers me.

"Sun, and sky, and breeze, and solitary walks, and summer holidays, and the greenness of fields, and the delicious juices of meats and fishes, and society, and the cheerful glass, and the candle-light, and fireside conversations, and innocent vanities, and jests, and *irony itself*,—do these things go out with life?"

For the saint, even, it will be a salutary exercise to reflect that his own success in detaching himself from the things of earth may not have been complicated for him by a mind with such subtlety and wistfulness in perception as we have here. Not all who aim at perfect detachment have to take pains to wean themselves from the greenness of fields, or to put from them a sense of the security of streets. How many in completing the victory over self have numbered *irony* amongst things given up, or thought of it as a thing at all? How many have thought of it as a created gift that might go in the same list as the juices of meats?

In all that last discourse to the Apostles Christ was allowing for human reluctance, allowing for the difficulties faith experiences in throwing its bridges over into the future. It was what he had been to them that was filling their thoughts. They seemed not to be able then to open their minds to the things promised. They were capable of only one thought. To preserve the companionship they had known they would have laid their ineffectual finger upon the spoke of the great wheel.

"And yet I can say truly that it is better for you that I should go away . . ." How human the "and yet" is? What respect for sadness there is in it. So complete is His sympathy with their dejection that He almost apologises for this alteration, though it will bring fulfilment of the great promise. He does not resent that the Apostles would set their ineffectual finger on the great wheel and 'reluct at the inevitable course of destiny.' He does not reproach them that they would hold back the coming of the Holy Ghost. Affected by their sadness, meeting it more than halfway, He pleads: "And yet I can say truly . . ." The great thing is not to miss that "and yet."